# Praise for *Tincture of Time*

"Compassionate, insightful, and witty! Schreiber-Mosher comes face-to-face with the realities of widowhood and emerges on a heartfelt path to personal growth. With wry humor and poignancy, *Tincture of Time* brings hope and practical wisdom to those on the road to recovery from the loss of a spouse."

—Constance Ahrons
Author of *The Good Divorce* and *We're Still Family*

"In *Tincture of Time*, Judy Schreiber-Mosher opens her soul to share the unfathomable depths of grief she feels in the wake of her beloved husband's death and the mysterious process by which she moves through it. Schreiber-Mosher takes readers on her personal voyage through unknown waters, reminding us that, while death and life are inevitably interwoven, love is transcendent."

—David Harte
Writer, *The Late Show with Craig Ferguson*

"I could not put this book down. . . . Schreiber-Mosher talks about the death experience of her husband and her own grief experience in a unique way that is both vividly real and hysterically funny! I encourage any widow or widower to put this book at the top of the list. It is through the telling of her real-life story that one gleans all the 'helpful tips for mourners' that are usually described in a grief self-help book."

—Robin Fiorelli, LCSW
National Sr. Director of Bereavement and Volunteers
VITAS Innovative Hospice Care

"*Tincture of Time* is more than a glimpse at one woman's grief process and her struggle to rebuild her life. And it is more than a guidebook for those suffering through their own loss and grief. It is also a love story—the love between the author and her beloved husband, and the author's love for herself. Love ultimately leads to healing, to rediscovering and embracing life. And that love is what makes *Tincture of Time* both extraordinary and important."

—Mike Foley
*Dream Merchant Magazine*

"Judy Schreiber-Mosher's passionate, pointed, and unsentimental account of losing the greatest love of her life touches the foundations of why we live and breathe, and reminds us that nature is fickle and our time on earth is borrowed from the great unknown. But even more than that, the book vividly displays

the wonders of a loving marriage, the kind of relationship that defies and surpasses even death."  —Peter Stastny, Psychiatrist
Author of *The Lives They Left Behind: Suitcases from a State Hospital Attic*

"*Tincture of Time* is a beautiful love story that continues long after one marriage partner dies and the other begins to move on alone. It is also a wise, sensitive, and generous investigation into what Schreiber-Mosher calls the 'roller coaster of feelings' she experiences as she grieves for her husband and takes the first steps toward reshaping her life. Neither sentimental nor despairing, the book brings laughter, tears, and—most important—a sense of strength and hope, even in the darkest moments. Anyone who has ever loved another person or suffered loss will respond to this honest, compelling, and brave memoir."

—Francine Klagsbrun
Author of *Married People: Staying Together in the Age of Divorce*

"Unadorned, with cool humor and linguistic ease, the author articulates the unspeakable: hopes, thoughts, and fears in the face of the fatal illness of her beloved husband. There *is* a life worth living for those who are left behind."

—Peter Lehmann
Editor of *Coming off Psychiatric Drugs*

"This unique book is filled with breathtaking moments of self-experienced knowledge in what it means to become a widow. Widowhood encourages a deep awareness of the complications involved in suddenly being alone. Schreiber-Mosher's intimate memoir is a testimony to the truth of our human condition and its healing resourcefulness."  —Theodor Itten
President of the Swiss Association of Psychotherapy

"While acknowledging that there is no formula for grieving, Judy Schreiber-Mosher tells her story in a way that will have you crying and laughing. Her strength and bravery are inspiring. This is a must-read for anyone who has been touched by death—which is all of us."  —Kathleen Wilhoite
Actress, singer, songwriter

"This remarkable account verifies that widows can restore their spirit, fulfill their own destiny, and determine what needs to go or stay in their lives. You will read it 'cover to cover.'"  —Donna Limerick
Award-winning documentary producer, formerly with National Public Radio

# TINCTURE *of* TIME

## *Living Through Grief*
## *to Hope*

Judy Schreiber-Mosher

**SOTERIA PRESS**

SAN DIEGO, CALIFORNIA

Published by: Soteria Press
2616 Angell Avenue
San Diego, CA 92122
www.soteriapress.com

Editor: Ellen Kleiner
Book and cover design: Ann Lowe

Printed and bound in Canada on 100% recycled paper

**Publisher's Cataloging-in-Publication Data**
Schreiber-Mosher, Judy
        Tincture of time: living through grief to hope / Judy Schreiber-Mosher,
        –San Diego , Calif.: Soteria Press, c2010
            p. ;cm.
            ISBN: 978-0-9824023-0-6
            Includes bibliographical references.


    1. Widows–United States–Life skills guides. 2. Widows–United States_Psychology,
    3. Spouses–Death–Psychological aspects 4. Mosher, Loren R., 1933–2004–Death.
    5. Cancer–Patients–United States–Biography. I Title

HQ1058.5.US 537 2010        2009902631
306.88/30973–dc22            1005


10  9  8  7  6  5  4  3  2  1

*To Loren,*
*my first true love —*
*I am forever grateful for all the*
*time we shared on this earth*

# Acknowledgments

ALTHOUGH I BEGAN KEEPING A JOURNAL WHEN MY HUSBAND, LOREN, WAS diagnosed with cancer, the inspiration for writing this book was two courses at the University of California, San Diego—Writing the Personal Narrative and Writing the Memoir—both taught by Professor Tom Larson, who instilled in me the desire to explore and write about the feelings that accompanied Loren's death.

I also want to express appreciation to my classmates, whose critiques were always helpful. Additionally, I am grateful to Mike Foley, who read and reread the manuscript, offering suggestions and encouragement. Many thanks to my friends Constance Ahrons, Dan Byrne, Ellen Eichler, Jack Heinowitz, Robin Fiorelli, Kim Harlow, Connie Hillis, Randy Margolis, Karen-Lee Robinson, and Jay Shaffer, who read the manuscript and patiently provided advice and support. Thanks also to Christine Forester for her love and support, her critical eye, and pertinent marketing suggestions.

Special thanks to my "old same" and chief cheerleader Sue Simmons-Alling, without whose support I would have not gotten through the years of grief and without whose encouragement I might never have finished this book.

Further, I am indebted to my acupuncturist, Laurie Morse, whose treatments were helpful for stress relief, relaxation, and creativity.

I am also grateful to my therapist Bev Hamowitz, who, following Loren's death, empathetically listened to my experiences of grief, as well as to each chapter of this book, expressing the belief in me that provided a safety net for exploring the emotional unknown.

Thanks to Ellen Kleiner, midwife of books, and her staff at Blessingway Authors' Services, who made the production of this book possible.

Although my mother did not live to see this book published, her belief in me provided the necessary grounding for its emergence.

And finally, continued gratitude to Loren for the life and the lessons we shared—that life is not a dress rehearsal and that tincture of time can help heal grief—which continue to sustain me during difficult times.

# Contents

1   Secretary of Death   1

2   Supervisor of the Ashes   21

3   Accepting the Warmth   37

4   The Widow's Mantra   47

5   Braving a Bereavement Group   56

6   Confronting His Clothes   65

7   Daring to Believe   75

8   Going Ring Cold Turkey   84

9   Blindsided by Valentine's Day   93

10   The Penis Test   102

11   Blending Memories   112

12   Honoring Loren's Legacy   121

13   Quantifying Grief   132

14   Tincture of Time   139

# 1

# Secretary of Death

*When he shall die*
*Take him and cut him out in little stars*
*And he will make the face of heaven so fine*
*That all the world will be in Love with night*
*And pay no worship to the garish sun.*

—William Shakespeare

"JUDY, THIS IS A DEATH SENTENCE."

These frightful words initiate my journey toward widowhood, down a two-lane highway of denial and despair. Loren Mosher, my first true love and husband of sixteen years, has just been diagnosed with liver cancer and, being a psychiatrist, fully comprehends the dreaded implications of his diagnosis. It's hard to believe that we met almost thirty years ago when we both worked at the National Institute of Mental Health in Bethesda, Maryland, and since have had an extraordinarily romantic and supportive relationship.

At the time we met, Loren, a commissioned officer in the Public Health Service, was the first chief of the Center for the Studies of Schizophrenia. He was an outspoken psychiatrist who believed that relationships had more healing powers than medications. When his research project Soteria House, which used little or no medications to successfully treat people with serious mental illness, supported this belief system, he was marginalized by his peers and ostracized from his profession. Yet he never gave up warning about the dangers of medications and supporting client groups who agreed with him.

I was an occupational therapist who worked directly with the patients, helping them optimize their functioning and develop skills for daily living. I had secretly put Loren on a list of men I wanted to meet, although I wasn't sure how I was going to make that happen. Then we were both invited to the same parties two nights in a row—the beginning of Camelot.

Now, we're in our bright, familiar, comfortable kitchen, sharing, as we always do, the experiences of our day. Loren wears a light brown checked sports jacket, a mustard-colored V-neck vest over a tan shirt, and his favorite khaki cotton slacks, which always end up with olive oil stains after he cooks. He stands in front of the black-topped electric stove and stirs the stew meat with the old reliable but battered wooden spoon. I sit on the other side of the counter and chop onions and garlic, the assigned ingredients for the evening's meal. The bright, cheery fluorescent lights make a mockery of our life, which has just been irrevocably altered by Loren's declaration: "Judy, this is a death sentence."

"See, I told you your mother would outlive us all," he then says, referring to my ninety-four-year-old demented mother, whose grip on life seems stronger than any ship tethered to the sturdiest anchor during a hurricane. For that second, I laugh along with him, as the macabre humor assuages some of the pain. He looks up, his blue eyes twinkling, and adds, "You're going to be a merry widow."

My knife stops in midair. I place it on the counter, slowly walk to where Loren is standing, and put my arms around his shoulders—to steady myself or to give comfort, I'm not sure. I recall that Loren had seemed more tired than usual when he returned from his latest trip to Germany, where he talked about the successes of Soteria House. My body comes to a halt, but my mind jerks forward. *This is not supposed to happen. We're too young for it. I am barely sixty-two and Loren at seventy is so vibrant. I just completed my last semester of teaching social work students so I could be free to travel more with him, unrestricted by school schedules, and now this! I understand the old truism "Man plans and God laughs."*

Finally, as the thoughts run their course, intense heaviness settles into every inch of my body and tears start to fall down my face. I silently ask myself how I can help this man if I'm filled with such fear and despair. The answer creeps into my psyche: Stay in the moment—don't think ahead—*and support him on any path he decides to take.* This counsel, like advice to the lovelorn, makes sense but is difficult to follow. I become like a petulant child sticking her tongue out while stubbornly refusing to follow directions as I shout, "I don't want to be a merry widow!" Immediately I follow this outburst with the question of a subdued, frightened child. "What are we going to do?"

"We are going to live every day until I can't," Loren replies emphatically. Loren's eagerness to explore and enjoy life always captivated me. He introduced me to the wonders of travel, the merriment of sex, and the beauty of opera. His favorite T-shirt reflected his philosophy of life: "I may be growing older, but I refuse to grow up."

That night in bed, I twist and turn like an insect caught in a spiderweb, trying to get away from the day's events, even as Loren puts his arm around me and we settle into our familiar skin-to-skin snuggle. We skip the nightly ritual of putting on music. *Maybe just as well. I would probably pick out Mozart's* Requiem *or the score of* Schindler's List, *both beautiful and appropriate, though probably too intense.* I close my eyes but can't sleep. Although I'm exhausted, my mind continues its meanderings through our life together, like a silent river not knowing the final route to the sea.

When we first met at the parties, I was immediately attracted to Loren's dark longish hair, his bad boy image, and the aura of adventure he projected. I was thrilled that he talked to me, and when he smiled, the world lit up, or at least my world did. I was attractive as well, with my short curly hair, blue eyes, great figure, and dressed in sexy tight white shorts and T-shirt, both hand embroidered by me with yellow and orange flowers.

Drawn to him like a moth to a lightbulb, that first evening I ended up going to his house, carrying one daisy and repeating my version of the childish rhyme "He likes me, he likes me not." *Romeo and Juliet* was blasting in the background, and he, wearing a navy blue and gray Japanese kimono bathrobe, was dancing around to the music. Now I wonder if the cancer diagnosis will suppress his normally irrepressible spirit.

I turn my head and look objectively at this man whom I love. He is a heavy sleeper so he doesn't stir. I smile as I remember another night early in our courtship. Both of us had been married before; I had no children, while Loren had three from his first marriage—Hal, then eleven, Timmy, ten, and

Missy, seven. That night Loren was sound asleep on the living room floor, and Missy and I tried to wake him up. We kept screaming, "Fire, fire," but he didn't budge. I yank myself back to the present and see a tired older man with short gray hair but still intent on fully living whatever there is of his life. I try again to sleep as the twin wrecking balls of death and reality hang over my head.

The next day I fall into my Ms. Fix-It mode, my personal coping strategy when I feel helpless. I remind myself that I have been a social worker for fourteen years, since 1980 when I earned my master's degree from Howard University, and have helped many patients with devastating illnesses, such as schizophrenia or cancer, as well as families in crisis. Regarded as empathetic, intuitive, and sensitive to the needs of others, I know what to do in such critical situations.

I zoom into action to gather helpful information. I go to the Rite Aide Drug Store and buy two spiral notebooks with a manila pocket in front to hold extra papers. I give the red one to Loren, and I keep the blue one for myself. Then I call everyone I know to ask about liver specialists. I get many names, which I put into my notebook and also start keeping a daily journal of events and my feelings. In the moments I focus on such tasks, I feel like I'm doing something helpful and seem almost normal.

Loren fills his notebook with names of treatment centers culled from doctor friends around the world: City of Hope and Stanford University Hospital in California, the well-known cancer center MD Anderson in Texas, and the treatment centers in Germany—University Hospital in Frankfurt and Havelhöhe in Berlin. Although I sometimes resented the extent of Loren's travels necessitating considerable time spent apart, as a result of his worldwide lectures about his research he became friends with many like-minded psychiatrists, one of whom I hope will provide the name of someone who can end this nightmare.

That feeling is fleeting, however, as the new normal becomes a continuous ride on a roller coaster of feelings without the gleeful relief at getting off. I open the horrid door of reality, look in for just a second, and quickly close it. I'm not ready to face reality, especially the fact that my husband may die. I know I am a survivor: my dad immigrated to this country from Russia with his family, including my ninety-two-year-old great-grandmother. I know I have the necessary professional skills and respect to be able to obtain employment and support myself financially. I have fabulous friends, but without Loren who will support me emotionally and prompt me daily to fill my life with fun? The wrecking balls, death and reality, continue to hover over my head.

Two days after the diagnosis I insist on going to the oncologist with Loren, something I would never have done in the past as we always respected each other's medical privacy. The past, however, disappears in the miasma of raw feelings and medical jargon. I make it clear that in this new situation the issue is not negotiable. Loren nods yes even as I can see no in his eyes.

Dr. Lamb, wearing a short white lab coat, ushers us into his sunny office. It's April, and through the large picture windows I can see the slight buds of orange and yellow marigolds. The flowers and bright sunlight, like the fluorescent lights in our kitchen, remind me of a life we once had, filled with fun and laughter. *My first ski trip, my first artichoke, my first orgasm, my first experience smoking pot. Was there really a life before the diagnosis, or was that other life a figment of my imagination? If Loren does die, will the nightmare of his death eclipse all the good memories?*

I notice the scattered papers on the doctor's sizable cherry wood desk and the many photos on the wall. *Are these pictures of some of the people he cured?* We all sit down, the doctor behind his desk. I study the face of this man who holds our fate in his hands, relieved to see a kindness both in his manner and his brown eyes.

The meeting starts. I dutifully copy everything down, barely hearing every other word. "This is not good," Dr. Lamb concedes. Next time I tune in I hear "stage four liver cancer, not operable." I concentrate on writing things down so I don't have to feel. I become the secretary of death.

"There are children," I whisper. "What should we tell them in terms of how much time he has?" Tears fill my eyes, and I say almost to myself, "Actually, I also want to know that."

Dr. Lamb, his hands folded on his desk, says in an even tone, "The average survival time is one year. The usual range is between a couple of months and a couple of years. It just depends on the course the disease takes in his body." *Cancer—that disease no one talked about during my childhood. Mom's six siblings died of cancer, as well as two of Dad's siblings.* I am terrified as I sit there, praying to no one in particular that Loren's win in this lottery of life is a "couple of years" rather than a "couple of months."

Before the diagnosis we had planned two trips, one to Hawaii to work on the condominium we had purchased just two months before, and one to Paris and Switzerland. A second Soteria House, which replicated the original experiment, had opened in Bern twenty years ago and Loren had been invited to speak in mid-May at the anniversary celebration, where he would receive much deserved recognition for his work.

He wryly comments that this Soteria House is his first grandchild, and asks the doctor if we can go. "Definitely, as long as you feel well," replies Dr. Lamb.

I feel lighter, hopeful, without realizing right away that this actually reflects my denial of the reality of Loren's condition. *Maybe it's not as bad as I thought, even though Loren said it was a death sentence and the doctor just said it was "not good." But then why would he let us go if Loren was that sick?* It is not until after Loren dies that I clearly see the doctor was really saying, "Do what feels good while you still can." That night I write in my journal: "I am frightened, but will try to take one day at a time. I love Loren so much and feel helpless that I can't make it right."

Two weeks later we go to Hawaii for ten days to work on the condominium. When we bought the condominium, Loren's idea was that it would not be a permanent residence but our personal resort. He would "park" himself here for three months at a time and write about his work. My fantasy was that I would go to the beach and come back tan and relaxed. We would drink wine, take walks, listen to music, and make love. I would go back to the mainland periodically to check on my mother. And the kids and grandkids would perhaps come for a family vacation.

We hire a contractor and buy a 1986 rusty, baby blue, beat-up Cadillac to use when we return. *Will we return?* We spend hours at Home Depot making inconsequential decisions about cabinets, paint, tiles, and various appliances. We laugh, tease each other about our preferences, and easily make the necessary decisions. The sales clerk observes us and remarks, "You two seem to have so much fun. I've worked with lots of couples who almost kill each other during the decision-making process."

Loren and I look at each other and smile. We have heard this before. Perhaps it's because we were both the beloved youngest of our families and never had to fight much for what we wanted. Or maybe it's that we simply love and respect each other, thoroughly enjoy each other's company, and feel secure with no investment in proving anything.

After shopping we go to dinner at a local restaurant. The festive tables are covered with flower print tablecloths that match the coverings on the white wicker chairs. The frangipani and plumeria leis add sweetness to the air, and the colored lanterns provide a dusky atmosphere. Loren gently takes my hand and says, "If I die, the condo is yours to do with as you like. You can sell it, rent it, or keep it to use."

My bubble of denial bursts, the wrecking balls hover closer, and tears again fall down my cheeks. I shake my head. I cannot fathom that he will not be here to enjoy this condominium. I don't know what to say. *What will I do if he dies?*

Several weeks later we go to Paris. I wonder how, under these circumstances, I can enjoy one of the most romantic cities in the world. I try to live in the moment. In our plush suite, we make love as if it were for the last time and don't talk about the future.

Then we travel to Switzerland, where we first visit Theo, a psychologist friend. While we await his arrival at a restaurant, I ask Loren, hesitatingly, "Are you going to tell him?"

"Yes, at the end of dinner. I don't want to ruin the evening," Loren assures me.

I dread that moment of revelation but meanwhile look forward to seeing Theo, who has a gentle manner but is like a big white bear with his shock of pure white hair, clear blue eyes, and pale skin. Using a blue fountain pen, he always signs his handwritten letters, "I send you a big bear hug."

"Theo, I have been diagnosed with liver cancer," Loren says softly at the end of the meal. "This may be the last time we see each other."

After his initial shock, Theo reaches across the mahogany dinner table, pushing the half-filled wine glasses aside, grasps Loren's and my hands, and we all give in to the sadness of this moment, tears on our faces. I am overwhelmed with a jumble of contradictory emotions: intense love for Loren, admiration for his honesty, and hatred of this moment, which, despite its warmth, signals death and endings.

We return from our trip and in mid-May start the process of, as Loren describes it, "applying to cancer colleges." In this application process, MRIs and X-rays take the place of SAT scores, which become the basis for rejection or acceptance into specific programs. I begin to feel as though we are one person, unable to separate the "he" from "me" as we together proceed down this path of facing possible cancer treatments in a way that supports hope.

We visit the City of Hope in Los Angeles. As we walk onto the grounds, I notice a building named after someone whose last name is "Mosher," which I see as a good sign. They are recruiting for a clinical trial of a new medication that has "tolerable" side effects: possible fatigue and anemia and such severe numbness in the extremities that the patient cannot hold anything hot or cold for at least three days after the treatment. We are told that the tumor is too big for surgery but if it shrinks through this treatment surgery may be possible. We go out to some raucous restaurant for dinner, and Loren says he wants to investigate all opportunities. I'm ready to make a decision, but it is not my decision to make. I write in my journal: "It is so difficult to focus on each day and try not to think further than that. I will feel much better when there is a plan."

At the hospital at my husband's alma mater, Stanford University, the oncologist advises him to go home, gather his children around him, and wait. We feel angry and frustrated. We return to our friend Connie's house in Palo Alto and, as we always do, sit around the familiar dark oak table under the mellow light of the Tiffany-style lamp. We smoke weed, get drunk, and enjoy one of the very special evenings that is savored only later. Loren mentions the many daily calls we are receiving from well-wishers and information seekers who feel like intruders to us. I suggest, "Let's get one of those multitasking answering machines where someone can press 1 if they want to know the daily report, 2 if they want the prognosis, and 3 if they just want to leave a message."

Then I have an even better suggestion: "How about if we code your health according to the Homeland Security plan and leave the color of the day on the machine?"

After my attempts at humor as a way to camouflage my deep concern, I silently apologize to my father for being horrified when, after his mother died, he and his brothers were laughing and telling jokes. Now, as an adult faced with the death of my husband, I realize that humor provides relief, if only for a moment, from the intense sadness that is always with me.

For Father's Day two of my three stepchildren come to visit: Missy, her husband David Lee, and their three-year-old daughter, Marley; and Tim and his wife Gretchen. I'm happy to see them, yet I don't want to share Loren. The men play tennis. Everything seems so normal on the surface, but it isn't. When at one point I walk into the kitchen to get knives to put on the table, I see my stepdaughter and Loren are crying.

"I love you, Daddy," she says.

"I love you too, darling," Loren replies movingly.

I wait a moment, put my arms around them both, and we all cry for several minutes before Loren returns to cooking dinner.

After resuming our search for cancer colleges, we have to face the fact that no one in the United States offers any hopeful interventions. Although we find there has been a lot of progress in cancer research and treatment, we are aware that liver cancer remains one of the deadliest forms of cancer. Drug treatments promise to prolong life, but since the duration and quality of that life are uncertain Loren is not interested. At the same time, Loren, a risk taker and man of action, tells me, "I can't do nothing." So on June 20 we leave for Germany, where he will participate in two experimental treatments: one in Frankfurt, involving delivery of electric shock to the tumor in hopes of shrinking it, and the other in Berlin, using mistletoe therapy to kill it.

We arrive in Frankfurt after a twelve-hour flight, weary and anxious. We check into a luxurious room at the residential hotel Mainplatza that has a small kitchen area in an alcove with the necessities for preparing a very basic meal: a two-burner electric stove atop a small refrigerator, a microwave, a one-size-fits-all frying pan, and simple serving pieces. The king-size bed faces a big window that opens onto a large square where colorful forest green, burnt umber, and plum red umbrellas shade the cafés and shops. I walk into the spacious, sensual black-and-white marble bathroom that has a deluxe bathtub, big enough for lovers.

I'm reminded of our trip to Venice, when we stayed in another luxury hotel, the Bauer Gruenwald, and spontaneously used the tub together after a night on the town. It had been my first trip to Europe, although Loren was a seasoned traveler. We had been dating for a year, and Loren joked that the best way to test a relationship was to travel together for three weeks. Our relationship passed the test as we ate and laughed our way through Europe, staying in Paris, Switzerland, and Venice, which became my favorite city. One night after sating our appetite with pasta and wine at Harry's Bar, we staggered back to the hotel and decided to take a bubble bath. As the tub filled with lavender-scented bubbles, we took off our clothes, carefully got in the tub one foot at a time, and laughed when it overflowed onto the mauve marble floor and flooded the bathroom.

We never use this tub in Germany. Instead, my life takes on a surreal quality as I make a home of our luxurious quarters in an effort to normalize our environment, in contrast to the traumatic experimental treatments Loren will face. Every day, I buy fresh brightly colored flowers and food, and establish a routine. Breakfast, then a swim in the Olympic-size pool while Loren rests; lunch, then a walk into town while Loren rests more; dinner at an Italian café and take-out for Loren, who eats very little. The night before the first treatment I write in my journal:

> *I am so hopeful that these treatments will help. I love him so much and do not like to see him in pain, either physically or emotionally. I feel like coming here was a very courageous thing to do — it is difficult being far away, but I will get through this.*

Just prior to the initial treatment Loren hunches over on the gurney, the white hospital gown barely covering him, as he signs American Express traveler's checks since Medicare is not accepted as payment. Overcome with the absurdity of the picture, I think, "American Express. Don't leave home without it." I am aghast at the way humor crept into my mind since there is nothing funny about the situation, but again I become aware that comic relief prevents me from total emotional breakdown.

As the treatment is about to begin, with electric shock directed into the tumor, the doctor tells me Loren is very sick and this is his "last chance." I am frightened as I wait for him to come out of the operating room. They wheel past me someone old and gray, and it isn't until the doctor says, "That's your husband," that I realize it is indeed Loren. In the ward, Loren, who never complained about previous medical procedures, says through clenched teeth, "I have never experienced so much pain in my life." I feel helpless, unable to offer hope or much consolation. We are relieved to return to the hotel but talk little and sink into an exhausted sleep for the next twelve hours. When we wake up, our world is changed forever. From this day on, Loren's condition seems to gradually but visibly decline as I watch in despair. Over the next few days, Loren becomes yellow. He hurts. His belly becomes bloated. I know I have to take care of myself, but all I want to do is watch over him and protect him. Yet I can't. My journal entry one day is revealing: "I am trying very hard not to take over too much because that is my tendency. Loren has no appetite—from the treatment or depression, or both?"

I drag out every coping mechanism I have. I swim every day. I call friends in the States. I try to remain positive in both thought and deed. I become nurse, wife, and caretaker. The wrecking balls hover ever closer.

Several nights after Loren's treatment I dissolve in tears and tell him how much I miss our ritual nightly snuggle. No matter how awful my day was, when he put his arm around me at night I felt sheltered and calm. Now when I need it most, there is no snuggle. I feel selfish for even mentioning it. I feel sad wondering if we will ever snuggle again. He apologizes: "I'm not myself." I feel guilty. *Jesus! Who the hell could be himself under these circumstances!* I am left with unmet needs.

The next day some magic enters our little world. We leave the windows open, and the sounds of our favorite Puccini arias float in from an outdoor concert. We lie on the bed and cry, feeling blessed and cursed at the same time.

The following morning the TV is showing *La Boheme*, one of the first operas Loren took me to see. On that day, at least twenty-five years ago, I drove my orange Karmann Ghia through a torrential rainstorm to get to his house. Loren had just stepped out of the shower, and I styled his long hair into a pageboy, using the blow dryer and my fingers. We made a great-looking couple as we took our seats. When the opera ended and we were both crying, we agreed that Puccini was for lovers and any chance we got we would go to a Puccini opera. Whenever we saw *La Boheme*, which was at least ten times, I would joke that maybe this time Mimi would live, but she never did. Now on top of the unmade bed we watch *La Boheme* again, but this time the opera begins to mesh with our own life, though with a gender role reversal. It seems like Loren is Mimi dying, and I am Rudolfo, the lover, helpless to save Mimi. I comment, "I am going to write a play about a couple who loved each other very much, who came to Germany for cancer treatments and one night heard in the nearby square their favorite arias, which reminded them of their love for each other and their wonderful life together."

*Will this be the last time we hear Puccini together, or will there be a future? I wish I knew. I'm drowning in a sea of sadness, yet I cannot. I have to be strong.*

After two weeks in the hotel, we go back to the hospital for the third time and the doctor tells Loren his health is precarious. He advises going home and waiting several weeks before making any further decisions. But Loren does not want to go home; he wants to go to the hospital in Berlin that offers the other treatment protocol, mistletoe therapy.

Loren, wearing his checked brown jacket, mustard-colored vest, and khaki pants, is silent as he puts his other clothes in the suitcase. He will not let me help him. I'm crying and angry as I throw my clothes in the valise, even as I realize this is no time to have a temper tantrum.

"What are you crying about?" Loren asks.

"I'm afraid you'll get worse," I confess.

"Could be," he answers, and with that we move on. *Where does Loren get his strength to face life head-on? Is it because his mother died of breast cancer when he was nine? Where is his sadness and anger?*

Our friend Volkmar, Loren's colleague from Hamburg, drives us to Gemeinschaftskrankenhaus Havelhöhe, the hospital in the suburbs of Berlin that utilizes both Western and alternative medicine. It's a warm day; the blue sky is without clouds. I notice a gift shop on the roadside

displaying brightly colored birds, cows, and other wooden objects hanging from a pristine white door-frame. Then as Volkmar turns in to the
hospital grounds, I see an assortment of cement buildings in the midst
of grassy fields scattered with beautiful red, lavender, white, and yellow wildflowers, seemingly offering hope amidst the dreariness of our
circumstances.

Loren is assigned a room on the ward, and I am given a room at the
guesthouse. I go to my small, clean unit with a single bed and private shower,
a room that surely belies the stories it holds. *How many other men or women
have gone to sleep in this room while their loved ones battled cancer cells? Will these
treatments be as painful as those in Frankfurt? Will they help Loren or worsen his
condition?* I force myself to unpack, trying to maintain some sense of order in
what feels like a disorderly life. I feel both fearful and hopeful anticipating
the treatment.

When I arrive at the ward, Loren is sitting on a scale, and to my surprise,
his eyes are twinkling in a way I have not seen in a long time. I comment and
ask why. His lips curve upward in a broad smile, and he says "nonspecific
factors," a reference to a research study that showed factors such as humor,
kindness, and a positive context all contribute to the well-being of a patient
and enhance any intervention being used.

As I leave the ward, I cry at the vision of Loren looking so small in his
hospital bed. This is the man with whom I have shared my life for the last
thirty years, but now I feel alone. The wrecking balls, death and reality, move
an inch closer.

The next day Loren begins treatment. Mistletoe therapy uses toxins from
the mistletoe to attack the tumor. The phrase "the kiss of death" comes to
mind, and I reflect on the irony. We tell jokes as the fluids enter Loren's body.
He good-naturedly chomps on the wheatgrass he has been given. Since the
unusual has become usual, it seems like a normal day. I knit, trying to keep
my mind focused on something other than death. Loren dozes off, and I am
comforted by his familiar loud snores. We chat on and off about nothing in
particular, occasionally holding hands without saying anything. Then I ask
Loren if I should call the children and tell them to come to Germany. "No!"
he responds emphatically.

Night comes. Loren puckers up for a good night kiss. I beg him, "Loren, please fight as hard as you can. I love you and need you so much." I start to cry. Tears well up in his eyes, as he says, "I love you, too."

"The nights are difficult, aren't they?" I say as I contemplate walking back to my room through the darkened shadows of the hospital grounds.

"Yes," he replies.

I want to crawl into bed with him, hold him, and feel the warmth of his body, but I slowly leave the ward. I have learned, over our years together, that Loren needs a lot more space than I do, and sometimes, despite my needs, it is better to let him be. I intuitively know this is one of those times.

Looking back on that moment I now know we were saying good-bye, both of us realizing in some part of our souls that he was not going to beat this.

I go to my room, get into the child-size bed, and fall into an exhausted sleep. The next morning when I return to the ward his nurse rushes up to me and says, "There was an emergency last night! He had an esophageal bleed."

I stop listening and wonder if this is it. But the nurse continues, "It was successfully repaired in the middle of the night. He's resting now." *Maybe my intuition was wrong, and I should have stayed last night. If I had been here, would it have made any difference?* Doubts and guilt swirl through my head. I push them away and try to attend to the moment.

I go into Loren's room and touch him, but he doesn't move. I see the entire outline of his shoulder bones as if they are covered in tight yellow leather. *Is this what is meant by wasting away?* I feel sick. He remains in a deep sleep most of the day. I sit near the bed, feeling useless, not even swatting the familiar flies. Toward the end of the day, the doctors realize his kidneys are not working properly, and I leave the room while they catheterize him. As intimately as I know Loren's body, I feel the need to respect his privacy during what seems like a very personal procedure. I soon return to my chair near the bed, and suddenly Loren sits up, saying, "I have to pee, I have to pee."

Trying to maintain my composure, I say, "Honey, you have a catheter." But his cry, like a sheep bleating, continues. I laugh and cry at the same time, feeling that I can't even calm my own husband. I ask the nurse for help.

Later that same afternoon Dr. Frankel, head of the oncology program, tells me Loren's kidneys have stopped functioning and asks permission to prepare him for dialysis. "Go sit with your husband. See if you can feel what he would want you to do," he advises.

I go back to the room, now still except for the sounds of suffering from the other rooms. The sun is sinking and there are vague shadows on the wall. I hear Loren's breath, but he is not responsive and I don't pick up any psychic vibrations. *Shit, how am I supposed to make this decision?* I recall that when we signed our wills, we both expressed our opposition to procedures that would prolong existence but not quality of life. I had little experience with death, but Loren, who had watched his mother and father die of cancer, knew the suffering it involved. I, on the other hand, never thought I would actually have to make such a decision. I take a deep breath and know I have to give permission for the dialysis because any promise of better functioning supersedes the previous agreement.

Magically Loren wakes up at the moment he is being wheeled out of his room to the ICU. I keep up with the gurney. My words come out in a rush. "Honey, your kidneys have stopped working, and I gave my consent to dialysis. Do you want to proceed with that?"

He nods his head yes. *Phew, not alone on that one.* Fortunately, the procedure is successful. After bringing dinner to me, the doctors urge me to conserve my strength and go back to my room to rest.

Before leaving, I am faced with yet another tough decision—whether to honor Loren's wish or call the children and tell them to come to Germany. Decision making was always easy when we did it together. But now, when I have to make what feels like momentous decisions that will affect all of us, I have to do it alone. If I don't call and Loren gets worse, or dies, I risk the permanent wrath of the children. If I do call and Loren improves, I risk his anger—an impossible situation. I make the decision according to my gut feeling. I call the children and tell them, "Your dad has taken a turn for the worse. You need to come to Germany." I finally go back to my room and write in my journal:

*Loren in ICU—I stayed until 1:00 a.m. not helping anybody—Loren pulling away when I tried to touch him—I decided it's better for me to get some rest, and maybe without me there he can rest, too—I'm exhausted—I love him so much, and I know he knows that and he loves me, too. Tomorrow will be difficult with the children coming, but one step at a time.*

I try to sleep but just twist and turn. One minute I'm hot, the next I'm shivering. I finally fall into an agitated, dreamless sleep.

The next morning Loren sits up in bed "bright eyed and bushy tailed," a phrase he would often apply to me when I woke up particularly talkative. I go to kiss him, and he puckers up his mouth. What a gift! He is his playful, mischievous self.

"Did you have a good night's sleep?" I ask.

"Yes, how about you?" he responds in a clear but soft voice.

"Yes. The kids are coming today," I confess.

"Oh boy," he says with some of his old humor. My hopes soar. *Maybe it is possible to beat this after all.* The wrecking balls, still there, recede just a little.

The kids miraculously meet in the Berlin airport: Hal from Marin County, Missy from Los Angeles, and Tim from New York. They arrive at the hospital late in the afternoon. Loren responds to their greetings with a weak smile and a verbal quip. Just a few minutes of conversation wears him out. Volkmar also arrives and suggests that we take the children out for dinner to give them some time to assimilate what's happening; last time they saw their dad was on Father's Day, when he promised he would "be back soon."

I want to stay with Loren, although I know it's a good idea to go. I tell Loren, "Volkmar wants to take us out to dinner so the kids can acclimate a bit."

He nods yes. I wish he had said, "You stay, but tell them to go." I want to be needed.

We drive to a cozy Italian restaurant, but the food sits on our table barely touched. We go back to Loren's room to discover him throwing up blood and writhing in pain. Suddenly it hits me more forcefully than ever before: he is dying. The wrecking balls, death and reality, are lowering.

"Is my husband going to die tonight?" I ask the doctor, my voice not even a whisper.

He walks our family into another room and acknowledges that as a possibility. We decide to take shifts, sitting by his bed.

Missy knocks on my door at 6:00 a.m.

"I've been with Dad since two. I think you should go down there now. He's very restless and wouldn't let me touch him."

Wanting to look good for Loren regardless of his state, I take a shower, put on a nice pair of black pants and bright shirt, brush on my makeup, and proceed to the ICU. I immediately notice that his vital signs are very low. Naively, I point it out to the nurse, who acknowledges it and puts some quick-fix medication in the IV tube. As his vital signs rise, so do my hopes. Although he is breathing very heavily, I feel some relief. Blinded by the mischievous duality of hope and denial I lean over and ask him, "Do you want to go home?"

"No!" comes the answer from somewhere deep inside of him, an eerie timbre to his voice. He continues to breathe heavily, as though climbing up a hill or having a fight.

I gently put my hand on his back.

"Uh-uh!" he says.

I think I am hallucinating. Once more I put my hand on his back and once more I hear "Uh-uh."

I feel rejected and angry, upset by a familiar conflict in our relationship: my need to comfort and feel close to him and his need for distance. But finally I get it. I go to the side of the bed, lean over the bars, put my face close to his ear, and say, "Honey, I know you always said you live alone and die alone, so I understand that. If you feel like you have to go 'giggling into the sea' (a phrase from a Tom Robbins book we used over the years when referring to how we wanted to die), then I'll understand. I want you to know how much I love you and what a special marriage we had."

I move back but stay very close to the bed. He dies about two minutes later, peacefully and naturally. He is with me one minute and then — poof! — gone the next. I now understand why people talk about death as crossing to the other side. I feel privileged to be present for this transition but numb and abandoned. Although Loren actually started leaving me as soon as he received his diagnosis, the permanence of his leave-taking is now undeniable. The wrecking balls of death and reality have finally crushed my hopes.

The children come in. I say simply, "He's gone." At that moment I have nothing left to give. They throw themselves on the bed. I feel small comfort when the doctor puts his arms around us as we cry. We stand intertwined and still except for the choked sounds of tears.

The doctor then tells us that it is the belief of the hospital, based on the philosophy of Rudolf Steiner, that it takes three days for the soul to move backward through the body. "During these three days, your husband's expression will change depending on where his soul is. Observe his facial changes and talk to him about all the positive as well as negative experiences you shared," he advises.

The children leave the hospital room. The nurse tells me to take as much time as I need. When I am finished, she will "prepare him for the chapel." I worry that Loren will be put into a black pin-striped business suit. Still in shock and pain, I stay with him for about thirty minutes, depositing his every feature in my memory bank, gently caressing his face, now calm and without pain, closing the eyelids on his blue eyes, running my hand over his unshaven chin, and smoothing his silvery gray hair.

Although the chapel is ours for the next three days, we need to get the key to it from the nursing station. The silver key, which hangs on a big wooden key ring, looks anonymous and innocuous, reminiscent of the keys for restrooms at gas stations that must be returned to the attendants. Yet the key to the chapel becomes the key to the reality of Loren's death.

To visit the chapel, we walk down several flights of stairs. Volkmar and I carry floral gifts in front of us like shields to protect us from the impact of why we are there, Volkmar a tall purple phallus-like flower that reminds him of Loren, I daisies in honor of that first night Loren and I spent together thirty years ago.

The chapel is small, with simple wooden chairs scattered around and one window that assures us there is life outside. Our eldest son, Hal, a Buddhist whom Loren always called "my spiritual self," sets up an altar, from which the pungent smell of incense permeates the space.

In the center of the room is a stainless steel bier on which Loren is placed. He's wearing a clean hospital gown, light blue speckled with spots of darker blue. It's hard to believe that just two weeks ago, also in a hospital gown, he was signing traveler's checks. A white sheet is spread over his legs. Beautiful sandalwood-scented candles surround the bier and there is a bunch of wild-flowers in his hands. I am amazed that he looks so relaxed and handsome, his famous grin on his face. I want to run and kiss him, but I'm constrained by the others in the room—the children and Volkmar.

Soon Tim leaves the chapel, saying, "J (Loren's nickname for me), I can't do this," and he returns to Los Angeles. Hal and Missy leave the next day, and Volkmar returns to his work. Then the chapel becomes my sanctu-ary. I visit often and stay long, talking to Loren about past events as if he were still alive.

I say, "Remember that Easter morning about a year after we met? We got up early to go to Easter Sunrise Service. 'Let's take some LSD,' you said. 'I only want a little bit,' I replied. We went to the park after the service and roamed around separately but together, the drug heightening our senses, acutely aware of each crunch of our feet and each dewdrop glistening in the shadows. On the way home, you were driving the BMW over a hundred miles an hour. I said, 'Loren! There's a police car following us. Slow down!' But instead you revved up to about a hundred and twenty miles an hour as we swerved through the park and lost our unwelcome tail."

I cry and yell at him, "About a year later I hated you when, while hosting a party with you at your house, I learned that you had gone to the ballet the previous evening with another woman. 'I can't do this,' I said and I broke up with you. The next morning you came to my door with the children and said, 'It's your decision, so you explain it to them.' I thought that was cruel, and yet I admired you for doing that. But then at three a.m., I heard you and your friend on my front lawn, pissing into the bushes. You kept calling and playing music to which we made love. It was six months before we got together again, and even then I told you I could only be a small part of your life because I didn't want to be disappointed again. I have to laugh, because whenever you saw me after that you would flash your Irish smile, your blue eyes would twinkle, and you would say, 'Hello, small part.' It drove me crazy."

During the three days, I watch Loren's wonderful smile turn into a ca-nine snarl, and I ask, "Where is your soul now that you look so angry?" I abruptly realize that I cannot ask him any more questions, and feel deep in my own soul the impermanence of life. *Who will give me my send-off?*

The last night I'm in the chapel I see his body rising from the bier. It's dark outside, and I think the candles are playing tricks on me. I always wondered what happened after death, but I am frightened by seeing my husband's body actually ascending to heaven. I cover his entire body with kisses, say my final good-bye, and run back to my room, through the wildflowers. The next morning I awake yearning to see Loren one more time before the coroner comes to pick him up. I race down to the nursing station, grab the key, and go to the chapel. It's light out now, and I still see his body rising! I'm no longer frightened, however, but feel comforted by the sight. I gently touch the wildflowers in his hands, drawing comfort from their freshness. As I force myself to leave the room, for just one moment I allow myself to face the awful fact that I will never see my husband in his bodily form again.

# 2

# Supervisor of the Ashes

*They told me, Heraclitus, they told me you were dead,*
*They brought me bitter news to hear and bitter tears to shed.*
*I wept as I remembered how often you and I*
*Had tired the sun with talking and sent him down the sky.*
*And now that thou art lying, my dear old Carian guest,*
*A handful of gray ashes, long, long ago at rest,*
*Still are thy pleasant voices, thy Nightingales awake,*
*For Death, he taketh all away but them he cannot take.*

— *William Johnson Cory*

"YOU ARE NOT THE BOSS OF ME!" LOREN WOULD SHOUT DURING ONE OF those familiar and often futile marital arguments that focused on control issues. But now I am. The boss of his remains. I have been promoted from Secretary of Death to Supervisor of the Ashes, another position for which I did not apply.

Volkmar and I wait for the coroner in the guest cottage. The room, which lacks adornment except for a drab tan card table supporting a speckled gray vase filled with faded orange and yellow artificial flowers, reflects our somber mood. Nothing feels alive, not even me. Although it is the middle of summer and the room has no fans or air-conditioning units, I feel very cold. Camelot is gone. I assume this is how Jacqueline Kennedy felt after the assassination of her husband: numbed by grief, yet having to make immediate decisions. I, too, must shove my grief aside and attend to "the arrangements" as they are euphemistically called.

The coroner walks into the room, wearing a black hat, black three-quarter-length coat (a morning/mourning coat?), black suit, white socks, and black wingtip shoes. *Are you for real? You look like you've been sent by Hollywood!* I clamp my mouth shut so my thoughts don't tumble out in words. Suddenly I feel like I'm in a Woody Allen movie in which life's most intimate and intense moments are presented with sardonic humor. Born and brought up in New York City, I always loved and identified with Woody Allen's films but never thought I would live a life worthy of one of his characters.

Herr Greve speaks no English, but fortunately Volkmar translates. "He wants to know if you are interested in cremation or if you want to bring him home in a coffin?" The religion of my upbringing, Judaism, forbids cremation because of the belief that the body and soul are one. But since Loren was Catholic or, as he liked to call himself, a "lapsed Catholic," I will honor his wishes. When Loren was first diagnosed with liver cancer, and death seemed but a distant possibility, I'd summoned enough courage one day to ask him what he wanted.

"Loren wished to be cremated," I say with certainty, and yet somewhere in the back of my mind I have a fleeting nightmarish thought of Buchenwald and Treblinka.

We discuss the scheduling of the cremation. Herr Greve says, "There's a backlog of cremations, and it may take up to a week." I envision a long line in a busy delicatessen. I'm taking a number, and waiting for it to be called. Now I'm channeling Woody Allen! But it's easy to erase the image since there are no accompanying smells of kosher pickles or pastrami. Instead, I try to concentrate on what Volkmar is asking me.

"Do you have a copy of your marriage license?" I find it.

"Do you have a copy of your birth certificate?" I hand it over.

"Do you have Loren's passport?" I produce that, too, with each document becoming increasingly despondent about the finality of what I am doing.

Herr Greve, on the other hand, broadens his smile, having shown more and more teeth each time I gave him a document. We go through the excruciating details: he will pick Loren up at noon on Tuesday but cannot promise when he will be ready to go home. I feel like waving my imaginary delicatessen number in front of him, but I refrain and murmur, "Thank you." I am in a rush to return home, yet I don't want to leave this place that holds the final memories of our life together.

On Tuesday at noon, Herr Greve picks up Loren as planned, and calls on Thursday to announce that the cremation is done. *So soon?* I push away the painful and horrid image of Loren going through a fire and wonder if there is a soul, and if so where his is now. *Is it possible we will meet somewhere in the future?* The emptiness I feel cannot be filled by a belief system; I have none.

Herr Greve and I make an appointment to meet at the airport Friday morning at 4:45 a.m. I tell this to Dr. Frankel then write in my journal:

> *I will miss him so much, but I feel positive about being here — perhaps after all Loren chose where he should die — at a Soteria-like setting. It was so hard to let him go to get cremated, but it had to happen. I would love to take his grin with me.*

Now I must get ready to depart. I sit in the middle of my small room in the guest cottage and dump the contents of Loren's suitcase onto the wooden floor — socks, underwear, pants, shirts, a sweater, a jacket, shoes, ties, and his toiletry kit. I stare blankly at the items, unwilling to decide what to leave behind and what to take home with me. *What difference does it make? A part of me is missing, and no matter how many clothes I leave or take, Loren is still gone.* Somehow I can't just leave everything here. That feels too final, like giving up.

I finger each piece of clothing: his favorite khaki wash-and-wear pants that he wore when he told me of his diagnosis; his checked brown jacket that he wore the last time we went out, just five days ago in Frankfurt, when he said he wasn't himself; and the multicolored Missoni sweater I bought him for what turned out to be our last Christmas. Loren loved clothes, and I loved buying them for him. He was always so appreciative and not shy about strutting about in them — my personal peacock. I pick up the sweater, rub its rough texture on my face, and try to recapture the time when we had our whole future ahead of us. It seems so far away yet was only three months ago. I keep the sweater. Perhaps I will wear it.

I turn my weary eyes to the black Coach toiletry kit, its outside faded and covered with gray-white splotches from daily use, the inside filled with the intimate smells of Loren. I got it for him many years ago when I couldn't stand to look at the old beat-up kit he was using. I try to be practical and decide to leave some of the clothing but not the toiletry kit, a symbol of Loren and his travels. When he was home, the toiletry kit was always in its same spot in the linen closet. When he was gone, so was it. Now, paradoxically, it is here but Loren is gone.

My long journey home begins with a 3:30 a.m. cab ride to meet the coroner at the airport, where he will give me the ashes and help me through security. The last time I got up this early was just four weeks ago when we flew to Germany. It seems strange to be leaving without Loren, at least in his bodily form. *I don't want to leave this sanctuary where we shared our last moments.*

The cab driver drops me off at the airport at 4:15 a.m. It is dark, with no personnel anywhere. I feel like I am in a ghost town with only a few remains of civilization: some lemon yellow fiberglass chairs, a dim fluorescent light, and some outdated computer monitors. I fold myself into a chair and hope I'm in the right place.

At precisely 4:45 a.m. Herr Greve arrives and solemnly hands me what looks like a black freezer container approximately nine inches in height, six inches in diameter, and weighing about two pounds. I accept this gift of my husband's ashes and try to give him a grateful smile as tears run down my face and my broken heart feels beyond repair. *What will happen to me now? The past is but a memory, the future is unknown, and the present is filled with death and uncertainty!* He shows a letter to the security people and then gives it to me to carry in case anyone questions my package.

I walk onto the airplane in a trance and take my seat. Despite my sadness, there is a part of me that has an objective view of my bizarre circumstances, making it feel like another Woody Allen moment. *Where do I place Loren — on the floor in front of me or in the overhead bin?* This plain black bag contains sacred cargo and I want it close to me. I settle the bag on my lap and hold it tight during the entire flight. The bag becomes Loren, and I am now able to hold him in my arms and comfort both of us somewhat, although he cannot assuage my tears of grief. I would like to flail about and scream and moan as they do in many other cultures to express grief, but for now I settle for silent weeping.

In Chicago, I stumble off the plane and have to go through security again. I put my purse, backpack, shoes, and ashes into gray plastic trays and walk through the screening arch. I am startled when I realize that Loren has become just another piece of carry-on luggage. This is not a Woody Allen moment but one of agonizing torment.

The TSA guard, a big black woman, shifts back and forth in front of her monitor as if doing a dance. I pick up all my belongings and realize that the black bag has not come through, that she is looking at the ashes through her security screen! I know I should show her the letter, but I want to observe how someone else will handle these alien specks. Finally, she looks up with the saddest, warmest smile and says, "Is them ashes, honey?"

"Yes," I say, and start to cry. "I have a letter."

"That's okay," she says as she waves me on. This small, unexpected act of kindness makes the rest of the trip bearable.

I step off the plane in San Diego, ashes clutched in my hand, precious jewels from a faraway land. I walk in a straight line toward my waiting friends, Connie and Roy. I observe myself from some distant forest in my mind and notice that I am numb, as if sprayed with an invisible coating of Novocain. *How is it possible to feel such excruciating pain and then feel nothing? Is this numbness I feel the psychic equivalent of fainting? If our species is so advanced, why can't it protect us from death—a hand grenade randomly thrown into the middle of lives, destroying everything it touches?* On the ride home, I sob as I tell Connie and Roy about how desolate I felt surrounded by strangers on the plane, how after dozing I'd wake up and look for Loren.

The Novocain wears off a little as we approach the house, a dwelling now for one. My feet are heavy as I put one in front of the other and with trepidation walk up to the front door, as if afraid of breaking something by moving too fast. I open the door and see the spectacular paintings Loren and I bought in another lifetime in Verona, where we laughed and sipped aperitifs at the local bodega and became friends with the artist. But the paintings, with their once cheerful globs of oranges, yellows, and reds, now seem to reflect anguish, as if distorted by a carnival mirror. The once chic black coffee table and the black leather, stainless steel "floating couch" in the family room now seem morbid. We both loved and collected postmodern furniture, each piece carefully selected for a special place in our home. My eyes linger on Loren's beloved black leather Eames chair, where he sat to read the *New York Times* and watch the sports events he so enjoyed, particularly tennis and football. I remember when we first considered buying it, at a show in Palm Springs, California. I thought it was too expensive, but Loren's enthusiasm trumped my caution when he said, "Judy, this is not a dress rehearsal." Now I comprehend all too well the meaning of that remark.

I continue to look around. *What am I doing here, and where is Loren?* My brain knows Loren is dead, but my heart does not accept it. I try to focus on routine actions, remembering that what I usually do when I come home from a trip is take my bag into the bedroom. But this doesn't help because it makes me realize with agony that I will no longer share the bedroom with Loren. Then I check the mail as I do immediately after trips, but in it I already find dozens of sympathy cards from friends and colleagues around the world that I can't face yet. Overwhelmed, I decide to check the e-mails and discover more sympathy notes and two Web sites that have been instantly and miraculously set up so anyone whose life Loren had touched can write their stories. The Web site from MindFreedom, a psychiatric survivor group, states, "Psychiatric survivor movement mourns Loren Mosher, who was like a Schindler of Psychiatry." The Society for Laingian Studies dedicated a Web site "To Loren Mosher, whom we will remember forever, with love and thanks."

Every place I turn reminds me of Loren's death. I feel like a giant caged rat with plenty of room to move around but still trapped by my environment. I hear Loren saying, "Judy, you can't control the world." But I want to, especially now, when my life feels directionless.

Connie and Roy watch me try to get my emotional footing and, after twenty minutes, ask me what I want to do.

"Will you sit with me as I open up the ashes?" I ask. I know I cannot do it alone. I put the container on the coffee table. I sit on the couch in front of it, while Roy sits opposite me in the Eames chair with Connie next to him. I open the black bag I carried across the ocean and remove a stark, black cylindrical metal container about the size of a two-pound coffee can. There is a heavy tin cover on the top with engravings that say #116301 Mosher, Loren, *03.09.1933 (his birth date), +10.07.2004 (his death date), and eg 13.07.2004

(date of the cremation). Then in capital letters KREMATORIUM POTS-
DAM. My hands stop moving, suspended in midair. My body jerks back, as
I experience an involuntary convulsion at the word Krematorium, with its
ominous meaning for someone like me, who is Jewish. It conjures up images
of men and women who are but skin and bones, heaps of dead bodies, striped
prison clothes, furnaces, smoke, chain fences, railroad cars, screams. I shake
my head to get the images out of my mind. I cry for them, for me, for Loren.
Then I force myself to refocus on the task of opening the container.

I need an instrument to pry open the circular top, like removing the lid
from a tin of gourmet delicacies. I find a household screwdriver, such a mundane tool for this sacred task. I try to get the top off but can't, so Roy does it
and hands it back to me. I am startled to find the ashes in this container look
similar to ashes left in the grill after a barbecue or in the fireplace after the
embers stop glowing. Nothing intrinsic makes them Loren's, only my projec-
tion onto them. It is beyond comprehension that the contents of this can are
the only earthly remains of my kind, gentle, loving, twinkly blued-eyed Irish
husband.

In one quick motion, I clamp the top back on the container. I try to think
of the most sacred place in the house where I can put this ugly repository.
Wanting Loren as close to me as possible, I place it on my dresser, where I
can see it from my bed—no substitute for the warm body that always lay next
to me, holding me tight.

When Loren was first diagnosed with cancer, I asked him where he
wanted to be when he died. "I want to be everywhere. I don't want to be
cooped up in one place," he confided.

But I also knew from Loren's reaction to the death of a college friend that
he considered it important to have some fixed location where people could
go and mourn. "Unless I participate in some sort of ritual and see a concrete
symbol of someone's death, I don't believe it," he said after his friend's ashes
were scattered without ceremony. Five years later, when my father died, Loren appreciated the Jewish death rituals: the graveside ceremony in which
each mourner threw dirt on the casket, the seven-day shivah when friends

came to call and brought food, and the ritual mourner's prayer said daily for one year.

So after I return home I search for a cemetery where some ashes can be placed to memorialize Loren. I visit the military cemetery, which was too cold; the Catholic cemetery where his mother was buried, which had cracked gravestones; the Jewish cemetery in San Diego, which doesn't feel right; and the nondenominational cemetery in Palo Alto where his father is buried. *Shopping for cemeteries is definitely not like shopping for dresses. They can't be returned if they don't fit.*

After finally choosing a niche in a beautiful marble columbarium overlooking a creek in the Palo Alto cemetery, I feel relieved. The piquant scent of lavender wafts over the area. A curved stone bench, where I can sit with my thoughts and hear only the sounds of the creek, embraces the columbarium. It is near Loren's dad and his alma mater, Stanford University, and close to where he was born and went to high school. This niche will contain only a small amount of the ashes; the remainder will be scattered as Loren requested.

I meet with Robin, the pretty, young, curly-haired newlywed working at the cemetery, who confronts me with yet another decision.

"What do you want on the plaque?" she asks.

"Simply the Best," I say, this time certain of the choice.

"Do you want your name on the plaque?" (Save money, do it early, she advises). Since there is a space for two people in the niche, I decide at that moment I want to be cremated, despite my religion's prohibitions, and have my ashes placed here, too. I always thought I would be buried in my family's plot on Long Island. My mother once joked that she could "get Loren in" even though he wasn't Jewish. At this moment, however, Long Island feels far away and I want to be with my husband, even in death. This symbolism is important to me, even if there is no afterlife.

I have to bring some of the ashes to the cemetery for the inurnment. Since there is no book on how to transport ashes, I am on my own. I put the black container on my bed, get a gallon-size Ziploc baggie, and telephone my girlfriend Darci. "Can you please stay on the phone with me while I put Loren in a baggie?" I ask her. Tragedy and comedy clash as sorrow simmers just under the surface. After I transfer some ashes to the baggie, there are ashes everywhere, including under my nails and on my bed. I cry, then sing, "I've got you under my skin." Surely this scene needs to be incorporated into one of Woody Allen's movies. But the task is accomplished.

Several days later I put the ashes in my carry-on bag, pray that security does not question me, and fly to Palo Alto. When I proudly present my bag of ashes to Robin, she asks in disbelief, "You put the ashes in a baggie?"

"Yes, how else am I supposed to get them to you? What do other people do?"

"They put them in an urn," she replies.

"Well, no one told me that," I say. She places the ashes in a soft green velvet bag that will go into the niche. The inurnment is scheduled for September 3, which would have been Loren's seventy-first birthday. Since Loren always loved parties, the children decided it would be appropriate to celebrate his death on his birthday.

In August I have a memorial service for Loren at the Marine base in San Diego. Having retired from the Public Health Service, he was entitled to military benefits. The chapel, which holds over a hundred people, is filled to capacity with friends from San Diego and Washington, D.C., colleagues from across the country, fraternity brothers from Stanford, and mental health "survivors," as his clients call themselves. All speakers acknowledge Loren's unique contribution to their lives. The mental health clients give me a particularly moving proclamation, which reads, in part:

> *Mental Health Clients for Wellness and Recovery San Diego and the California Network of Mental Health Clients along with clients in other states in the United States and survivors worldwide would like to take this opportunity to express to you our sympathies on Loren's sudden death. We will feel this and be saddened by this for many years to come. . . . In Loren we had a voice that could stand up to corporate managed care or the lack of it, large pharmaceutical companies, judges, lawyers, and others. Loren had wonderful insight into*

*what a person needs to recover from a setback. . . . Loren's work will live on*
*in the many clients and advocates he befriended, supported, mentored, trained,*
*and stood by. . . . Thank you for supporting his many causes.*

The day after this service, the first dispersal of ashes is to take place at
the local café where Loren and seven other men met daily at noon, calling
themselves the "old farts club," a humble name that belies their accomplishments as a former chancellor of a university, a former editor of a big city
newspaper, famous architects, and nuclear physicists. Loren loved participat-
ing in their stimulating discussions, which focused on political or philosophi-
cal issues, operas, dramas, or other current topics.

That Sunday morning, I put a pint-size Ziploc baggie full of ashes in my
purse and go to the café with our friend Connie, here from Palo Alto for the
service. The patio is teeming with people reading papers or engaged in spir-
ited conversations as they sip lattes, mochas, or cappuccinos.

"How on earth are we going to do this?" I ask as I shift my eyes from side
to side and my hands fidget with the silverware at our table near some bushes.
*Wonder what the fine is for throwing human ashes on private property.*

"I'll establish a pattern of throwing crumbs to the birds," Connie says,
"and then we'll keep throwing except we'll mix ashes in." We do this successfully. I feel like an undercover agent who is staked out to make a drug bust.
Again it feels weird to be so bereft about a situation and yet still be able to
find humor in it. *How can I laugh when it is Loren's ashes I am tossing about?* Then
I remember that in my psychology classes we discussed the use of humor as
a defense mechanism. I understand that laughing is a way of dealing with my
grief, and I forgive myself.

It's a logical next step to throw some of Loren's ashes into the Chesa-
peake Bay in Maryland, where we sailed for twenty-two years prior to moving to San Diego from Washington, D.C., eight years ago. Loren, who had
owned several sailboats over the years, had taught me how to sail, especially
how to maneuver a boat during summer squalls when lightning lit up the sky
and rain poured down.

I fly to Maryland with a baggie full of ashes. Loren's best friend Larry,
his son Thomas, our friend Jay, Larry's wife Donna, and I drive to the bay on

one of those rare fall days when the cloudless sky is a brilliant blue and there is enough wind to put up the sails. A sudden gust of wind blowing orange, red, and gold autumn leaves off the trees reminds us of the continuous passage of time, providing the perfect backdrop for our task.

Larry, his skin a ruddy brown from sailing, steers his boat, *The Zephyr*, to a special spot where we had all shared adventures and anchors it. He takes a fistful of ashes and says, "Best buddy and coconspirator Loren," then stops midsentence, his voice choking with emotion. After a moment of silence, he checks the wind to make sure the ashes will go away from us, throws them overboard, and we watch them drift off until they are no longer distinguishable as separate from the bay. Next we take out some rum and tequila and tell stories about our treasured adventures, a ritual that makes Loren come alive.

Larry remembers the time we sailed to Maryland's Eastern Shore for the Fourth of July. It was getting dark and Loren was at the helm, wearing a favorite Grateful Dead T-shirt that read, appropriately, "In the shadow of the moon I know we'll be there soon." We were having a sundown cocktail and chatting when suddenly Larry shouted, "Loren, watch out!" As Loren looked up, the boat crashed into a buoy and the lines got tangled up. Loren yelled to no one in particular, "Quick, get the scissors," gave me the wheel, and he and Larry tried to untangle the lines as the boat continued to move forward, dragging the buoy with it. Not until we were safely anchored in a favorite cove several miles up the bay could we laugh about the incident.

Jay talks about the time we were in the Caribbean, took the dinghy to shore, and went to a fancy restaurant, remarking, "Loren was furious when he had to borrow a jacket from the restaurant just to get in. He looked like a miniature person inside this blazer that was so huge on him. But it was worth it. At the end of the meal, Loren, pretty tipsy and back to his normal size without the jacket, could barely steer the dinghy to the boat, laughing all the way and saying something about 'going giggling into the sea.'"

"Yeah," I say, "the only reason you remember that is because you took the dinghy back to shore to get laid, but before you were halfway there you turned around and came aside the boat, yelling, 'I forgot my condoms.' Loren, who was chortling remembering his own youth, found the condoms and, saying, 'Hope they don't have holes in them,' threw them to you."

Jay giggles.

Donna, recalling how we spent nights sitting on deck smoking, drinking, and laughing, comments, "Suddenly Loren is slumped over, sound asleep and snoring loudly. Each time we would try to wake him up, he would stare straight at me and then slump over again. After about twenty minutes, he made some semi-human sound, and Larry helped him down the steep stairs so he would not fall on his face."

I remember the first time we made love on the boat and how hard it was to position ourselves in the front cabin, the triangular-shaped fo'c'sle, or "fucksle," as Loren liked to call it. I keep this personal memory to myself.

Finally, Thomas, a devout Catholic, walks over to the starboard side of the boat and hands me a small wooden cross that was blessed in the Holy Land. He knows I'm Jewish, but he wants me to have it. This gentle gesture brings more tears to my already puffy eyes.

In October, three months after Loren's death, I fly to New York City to use our Metropolitan Opera tickets. I ask Loren's colleague and friend Peter to join me because I have learned that every "first" without Loren is difficult. Peter and Loren founded a group called INTAR (International Network Toward Alternatives and Recovery), but Loren died before its first meeting. I warn Peter that I will be putting ashes here and there inside the opera house. First, I rub some on our subscription seats in the dress circle. Next, at intermission, I order a drink at the bar, where we always had a glass of champagne, and put some ashes in the planter in front of it. Then, in what I think is a subtle maneuver, I sprinkle some ashes on the floor in front of our seats. When the person sitting next to me returns from intermission, he asks in a rather brusque voice, "What the hell did you bring in here, a beach?" I give him my best full smile and hold up my hands in an "I don't know" gesture. I am reminded of the Greek tragedy/comedy mask: in some moments I feel so sad, while at others I laugh about a situation of my own making.

I go to Hawaii in January, taking some ashes with me. I don't return to the condo we bought, which is now rented, but stay at one of the beautiful military bases on the island. I leave my little cottage on the beach and stroll down to the water, carrying Loren's ashes wrapped up in a tissue. I walk into the water and release the ashes without checking the wind direction. The ashes blow back at me like a soft eyelash kiss. *Oh well, it feels nice having Loren all over me again, just like the last time we were in Hawaii—even though then he was in the flesh and now just dust and a memory.* I brush off the ashes as I watch the gentle waves returning Loren to the universe.

As I plod day by day through the months after Loren's death, I'm surprised to discover that I want to travel, an activity that Loren and I both loved. I acquire every available travel brochure: glossy ones with pictures of soft green mountains and blue lakes, others featuring pictures of lions and tigers beckoning me to go on a safari, and still others with pictures of huge hard-backed turtles asking me to join a trip to the Galapagos. But despite the lure of places unknown, I find that I want to return to Italy, this time on a pilgrimage—to put ashes in some cities special to us, particularly Rome, where we had lots of friends, and Venice, which, since the bubble bath we shared, had been a place of romance on every trip to Italy.

In Rome, my small hotel is near the majestic Coliseum, with its ancient ruins rising into the air like gods from an unknown world. I walk down the same cobblestone streets where, in some distant past, bronzed men with golden shields and helmets waited on their horses for chariot races to begin. Gorgeous Italian women and men rush by, cell phones to ears, as they gesticulate with their free hands. In between the historical monuments are monuments of the current century—carts with hats and T-shirts.

I reach a small café where I am to meet our friend Roberto. I reflect on the first time I met Roberto, twenty-five years ago when Loren went to Verona to write a book about the new Italian Mental Health Law and Roberto was coming to Maryland to work at Walter Reed Hospital. Loren's Italian friend and coauthor, Lorenzo, arranged for a home exchange, and during those eight months I spent many nights with Roberto, drinking Glenfiddich and engaging in "deep communication," as he called it. Subsequently, whenever Loren and I went to Verona, or to Rome after Roberto moved there, we would visit him and continue our conversations enhanced by Glenfiddich and marijuana. My reverie is broken when Roberto suddenly appears, and with teary eyes I melt into his arms.

Lorenzo told Roberto of Loren's death, but he is interested in the details since he is a pathologist specializing in the liver. He is concerned that Loren might have had hepatitis and makes me promise to get tested when I return home. I tell him I have brought some of Loren's ashes to distribute here in Rome and then Venice.

Roberto pulls at his black mustache as he says, "Joody, could I have some? I would like to have my own private ceremony in my little garden. I will drink Glenfiddich like Loren and me did and remember all the good times we had in Verona and here." His face is all smiles. "I will watch carefully to see if any sinsemilla appears." I give him some ashes in a tissue, relieved that he does not think I am crazy.

After Rome I travel by train to romantic, magical Venice. *Will it still be romantic and magical alone?* I check into a hotel that triggers no memories of any previous trip.

The next day I go to St. Mark's Square, usually our first stop on any trip to Venice. There I order the ritual Prosecco while seated in front of the familiar Café Florian, where the musicians, in their white dinner jackets and black ties, play "Che Sera, Sera," an appropriate song for the moment. I watch the tourists feed popcorn to the pigeons that, as if on command, fly onto their shoulders for a photo op. I place some ashes under my table, where they blend inconspicuously with tourist detritus on the cobblestones.

I recall how during our first trip to Venice together Loren and I went to Harry's Bar, where the owner, Mr. Cipriano, recognized Loren, who had been there many times before, and cordially said, with hand outstretched, "*Buonasera, signor et signore. Come sta?*"

"*Bene, grazie e lei?*" Loren answered, impressing me.

Because we had smoked some marijuana and were enjoying each other's company, the world was sparkling and everything seemed hilariously funny. Our waiter, in a cream-colored dinner jacket and black bow tie, joined in our fun; every time he passed us as he carried food to other tables, he stopped and put a little on our plates, giving us our very own tasting menu.

It becomes more complicated to find a way to place ashes in Harry's Bar, as it is crowded. There's a woman in a gorgeous yellow silk suit sitting next to a mustachioed man in a blue blazer and white pants, clearly there to be seen. There are tourists in plaid Bermuda shorts and T-shirts straining their necks in hopes of getting a glimpse of some important person. But I do not want to be seen, nor am I interested in seeing people; and I certainly don't want to spend $18 for a Bellini, the bar's signature peach nectar and champagne drink. Instead, dressed for intrigue in my London Fog raincoat I focus on my secret mission to spread ashes.

I take a fistful of ashes with one hand and pretend to look for someone while I quickly drop the ashes on the floor. I can hear Loren telling his heaven mates, "That's my wifey. When she sets her mind to something, she does it." I smile as I think about that, but then my whole body slumps with intense sadness as I realize that I will never hear him say that again.

Next I contemplate placing ashes in the Canal Grande. Lorenzo and his longtime girlfriend, Mirella, come to Venice to participate. Lorenzo looks dapper, like the handsome lead man in a Fellini movie, with his once black wavy hair now turned gray, a rust-checked sports jacket, brown corduroy slacks, and matching bow tie. Mirella also looks chic, with her blonde hair framing her perfectly tanned face and wearing stylish gray- and green-striped stockings that match her green skirt, along with gorgeous leather Italian shoes and purse.

I want to rent a private gondola, but they convince me we should take the *traghetto*, a public gondola taxi that holds six to eight people. We board it along with camera-carrying tourists and the gondolier in his black-striped shirt and fancy straw hat.

Lorenzo and I look at each other and, as if on cue, grab a fistful of ashes to deposit in the canal. Mirella, her right leg high in the air, begins taking off a stocking to divert the attention of passengers, who gawk at her as they might a show in a girly bar, while we release the ashes. As the gondola gets closer to the other side of the canal, Lorenzo and I each rub our hands together in an effort to brush off the remaining ashes, but I cannot get them off my hands, Lorenzo holds his clean hands out to me and asks, "Why do the ashes stick to your hands, Judy, and not to mine?"

"I don't know," I say, as I consider possible cosmic explanations for this difference. *Are they sticking to me because Loren is sending some kind of message or because the bond between a husband and wife is stronger than that of a friendship?*

Back home, I reflect on how each time I place ashes somewhere, I let go of Loren a little more. Now I reconsider where to put the ashes I have left in the house. I decide to place some in a little mint-green silk purse mixed in with my Victoria's Secret bras and underpants, a place I know Loren would like to be. I place the big black container, now only half-filled with ashes, in what used to be Loren's closet so I don't have to look at its starkness every moment. I have been told that ashes make wonderful fertilizer, and I fleetingly think about making a planter out of the ugly container, but that idea does not seem to fit Loren's character. Keeping the ashes in these places feels right, but I am learning that grief is a fluid situation, that my feelings change daily. And I realize that regardless of where the remainder of the ashes rest, there is no way I can ever make Loren's death right.

# 3

# Accepting the Warmth

*Sometimes our light goes out but is blown into flame by another human being.*
*Each of us owes deepest thanks to those who have rekindled this light.*
—*Albert Schweitzer*

"WHAT WILL HAPPEN TO HER? YOU BETTER TAKE CARE OF HER," DONNA, LARRY'S
wife, questioned and lectured Loren simultaneously, one hand around my
shoulder, the other shaking at Loren. "You're taking this girl away from her
friends, from her support," she continued, her voice rising as her eyes filled
with tears. It was the day we moved to San Diego after Loren had been hired
as Director of Mental Health for San Diego County.

"I'll be fine," I told Donna that day. "It's just another adventure like our
sailing trips. There will be some bright sunshine days and, I'm sure, some
squalls." It never occurred to me that the squalls would come in the form of
Loren's cancer diagnosis and death.

Why did he have to die? The question, poignant in its simplicity, has no answer. There seems to be no immediate salve for the gaping wound of emptiness
and sorrow, even though Connie and Roy are in my home trying to comfort me.

"I think we should get something to eat," Roy says. Connie nods her head.

"I'm not hungry," I tell them. Although food is furthest from my mind, I
do recognize the need for sustenance and say, "Okay, let's go to Piatti." Piatti
is a neighborhood Italian restaurant where Loren and I had a special rela-

tionship with the handsome, dark-haired, young manager, Jason. Loren, a wine connoisseur, always brought a special bottle of wine to drink with our dinner. The first time we did this Jason came over to challenge Loren on his choice of wines, and when Loren offered him a tasting glass, a serious discussion about grapes ensued and a friendship was immediately cemented. Thereafter, every time we ate at Piatti we would share some wine with Jason and exchange anecdotes about our personal lives.

"Are you sure you want to go there?" asks Connie, "It holds so many memories."

"Where won't there be memories?" I reply, my tone sharper than intended. *Why have I chosen this restaurant when it could bring more pain?* I realize that I probably chose to go to this restaurant, which Loren and I thought of as "our place," because I need something familiar to anchor me in the moment, an emotional teddy bear.

At the restaurant, Jason hugs me and asks the usual questions: "How are things? Where are you returning from now?"

I want to answer, but I'm unable to form any words.

Connie fills in. "Judy just came home from Germany, where Loren died."

I look around the restaurant and see all the familiar things—the tables with fresh flowers, the hard-crusted bread with the grainy, brown oil and garlic tapenade, the waiters in their dark pants and white shirts, and the happy chatter of the clientele. *How can the world go on so normally while I am experiencing such turbulence in my life?*

Yet the fact that the restaurant is still the same despite Loren's death is reassuring. I sit in the same tan rattan chair I sat in when Loren was alive and feel safe and comfortable. I order my usual comfort food—a margherita pizza and a side order of spinach sautéed in garlic and oil—along with a bottle of wine. Jason comes over with a plate of warm garlic green and black olives and suggests we make a toast to Loren. "To Loren, a friend, we miss you," Jason says, as we raise our glasses.

He goes back to his other customers, and we resume our meal. The sky is falling, and we talk about the weather in San Diego and the amazing fact that I got upgraded on the trip home. At last the meal is over, and we signal for the check.

"Not to worry," Jason says, "I am taking care of it."

I'm grateful for this bright star that appears on my horizon, this gesture of kindness by a friend who recognizes, and shares, my loss.

When we return to my home, Roy gets up to leave and Connie says she is spending the night. I mouth the usual "Not necessary," feeling the difficulty of accepting the warmth and support of friends even as I need it. I want to be alone, and yet I don't. I want to feel, and yet I don't. I go off to bed, alone.

The act of getting into bed alone, like a pail of ice-cold water thrown over the head, shocks my system into heightened awareness of a past experience when Loren and I were snorkeling off our sailboat in the bright aquamarine waters of the Caribbean. He had already gotten to shore, and I was still swimming, struggling to catch my breath and make headway. Finally, in a panic and short of breath, I yelled to Loren, "I can't swim anymore. I don't think I can make it to shore!"

"Put your feet down and walk!" he yelled back.

I put my feet down and sure enough was able to walk to shore. Now I'm not certain I'm going to make it either, but there is no one to yell, "Walk!" Or is there? *When friends like Connie and Roy, and even Jason, reach out and offer support, is that the equivalent of Loren yelling, "Put your feet down and walk"?* I huddle on my side of the bed, try not to panic, and finally fall into a restless sleep.

Miraculously, one day follows another, days of trying to cope—with the mail, the bills, the children, my life. I struggle to get my emotional feet on the ground, but the ground keeps shifting and I can't find a comfortable place to stand.

One day my friend Robin, director of bereavement for a hospice corporation, comes over with a bag full of groceries and a stack of books on grief, which she's gotten from the hospice library. I had seen movies in which, when someone dies, friends bring over food and supportive gifts, but I never expected to be the recipient of such kindness so early in my life. I look at the stack of books but am not ready to face my grief in such a stark, realistic way as reading books on the subject. Even so, I appreciate Robin's care, which they reflect.

Then one evening for dinner I meet my friend Karenlee, whose husband died exactly one year before Loren. Looking pretty, with her stylish gray hair set off by a lavender suit, she gives me a stack of xeroxed articles on grieving.

The mountain of reading material on grief near my bed keeps growing, like the beanstalk in the fairy tale, higher and higher to the sky. But I find no comfort in it, only reminders of my grief.

Before I go to bed each night, I listen to telephone messages, jot them down, and then ignore them. I peruse the Web sites with their tributes to Loren; these become my personal bedtime stories that bring me closer to him, making me feel that he is giving me a virtual snuggle. An entry from the son of our friend Theo, whom we met in Switzerland, reads:

> As the son of Theo and Heidemarie, we visited Loren and Judy in America a few years ago. I felt the positive and warm atmosphere in your house as we were having dinner together. Loren's humor and hospitality was heartwarming and will stay in my memories. Judy, I wish that in every breath of you, the good energy of Loren will give you strength.

Lorenzo, Loren's colleague who met me in Venice, writes:

> Loren is one of the great men of our age in the fight for human rights and dignity in psychiatry and beyond. His greatness and his role and importance as one of the fathers of the mental health movement will be more publicly recognized and acknowledged when ostracism by his contemporaries of the psychiatric establishment will give way to the justice of history. He paid a high price for his unconditional advocacy in favor of the client, his love for truth and justice. Thanks, Loren, for teaching us what psychiatry is, or should be. We will treasure your legacy forever.

And there are touching tributes from former patients:

> Hello, Dr. Mosher. I prayed for you. Now you're going over to the heavenly world. Maybe the corrupt doctors will try not to remember you, but we, the survivors of psychiatry, will certainly remember you. I wish those you leave behind, family and friends, a short mourning period and strength.

The bedtime tributes help at night, but the days are almost unbearable. I'm stunned that I find it so difficult to perform even rote tasks that in the past were so easy to accomplish. I aimlessly pick up a pile of papers from the table and am shocked to find so many unpaid bills, as if the few that I knew were there somehow multiplied overnight. I have never been behind in paying bills, but I can't get organized.

My good friend Ellen calls and tells me, "I have put aside three hours every Wednesday afternoon for you. You can use me any way you want." Can you do magic tricks and bring Loren back? I almost ask. Yet this gesture is another bright jewel to put on my invisible bracelet of life's kindnesses.

When she first comes and I ask her to help me with my bills, I'm so embarrassed. For several hours, she opens up bills, tells me how much they are, and I write checks for them—the sort of excruciating process I, an occupational therapist, would do with someone who had minor brain damage. Although my brain damage is invisible, caused by one of life's sucker punches, I am just as dysfunctional.

Other friends also keep stopping by to check on me. Their presence makes the house less empty. My social work colleague and friend Linda wisely comes with two brown, crinkled paper bags filled with coffee beans, saying, "You will need these as people drop in to see you and want a cup of coffee." And Kumi, who helped Loren and me organize our lecture tour of Japan, where he talked about Soteria House and I talked about case management with psychiatric patients, brings a lovely whipped cream cake, its top studded with bright red strawberries and blueberries. Each kind gesture feels like a warm breeze floating over my persistently cold body.

The cards also keep coming in. I put them all in a pile knowing that one day I will do the correct Emily Post thing and answer them. Several months later when I reread them, I have no memory of having seen them—testimony to the numbness of initial grief.

I go to see Bev, my caring therapist of three years, and tearfully recount my experiences in Germany and read the quotation from *Romeo and Juliet* that I want to use on the program for the memorial service the children and I decided to have one month after my return home. *How do I plan something I don't want to happen?* I talk about how much I miss Loren, how I feel overwhelmed with everything, and how I cannot conceive of a future without him. She reminds me that all I have to do now "is put one foot in front of the other," soothing advice that mirrors Loren's earlier advice on the sailing trip. I cry the whole session and notice she also has tears in her eyes.

At the end of the session, she says, as I take out my checkbook, "I'm not going to charge you for this session."

This is another small kindness that reminds me of the goodness of humanity. Suddenly I feel as though I will not have to traverse grief alone, that others will walk this road with me.

I investigate various venues for the memorial service but none seems right. Over the phone, I consult about the service with Sue, who has been my best friend since we met twenty-nine years ago, when we both worked on the same ward at the National Institute of Mental Health.

"Judy," she says, " Loren is retired from the Public Health Service and is entitled to use the chapel on the Marine base. Why don't you investigate that?"

Brilliant! I go there and find the secretary who is in charge of planning funerals and memorial services — Mrs. D, as she calls herself — a relic from the 1950s. About fifty-five, she wears shiny, black patent leather high heels, a dark skirt just above her surprisingly shapely knees, and a flower print blouse. Her long nails are polished blood red, and her bleached blonde hair is styled in the bouffant fashion of a 1950s housewife like Lucy from the *I Love Lucy Show*. But Mrs. D is kind and competent and helps me plan the service I want for my husband. No question is too silly to answer and no task too difficult to accomplish.

"I'd like to bring several CDs, Beethoven's *Eroica*, operatic love songs, and a special rendition of 'Ave Maria.' Is that possible?" I ask. I know Loren would want *Eroica* because every time we listened to it he would say, "This is what I want played at my funeral." I think of the operatic love songs as a tribute to both our love and our love of opera, and the "Ave Maria" as a soulful arrangement we both loved.

"No problem," she says, "I will assign an officer to take charge of the CD player."

"There may be over a hundred people here. Will there be room for all of them?" I ask.

"Absolutely," she answers.

Then Mrs. D tells me that Loren is entitled to a twenty-one gun salute and asks if I have the flag necessary for such a ritual.

I have no idea what she is talking about. She gives me numbers to call, and again I feel like a caged rat, but this time trapped in a bureaucratic maze of unbelievable proportions. Everyone I call says Loren is not entitled to a flag, for if he were, he would have received one when he retired, and so we go ring around the rosy until I almost fall down. But since I want this service to be right, determination overcomes my grief, and I persist. Finally, I reach the officer in charge of military dependents at the naval base, and when I tearfully tell him my problem he offers, "Why don't you come down here and let's see what we can do."

Once there, I am greeted by a tall African American man with kind hazel-colored eyes, whose appearance soothes my anguished spirit before he even says a word. He hands me a flag with woven blue background and white stars and stripes appliquéd over the blue, and folded in a perfect triangle. I recall JFK's funeral when, after the ceremony, Jackie was presented with a flag just like this one. It feels sacred, both for our country and for me. I hold the folded flag in my lap carefully as we talk for a while and find out we are both from Washington, D.C., making me feel that a neighbor is helping me.

The memorial service is a triumph, if that word can be used to describe the commemoration of an event I don't want to recognize. I remember being shocked that after my father's funeral my mother seemed pleased, remarking, "Dad would have really liked this."

Now, eighteen years later, as I sit through this service that I planned from the first piece of music to the twenty-one gun salute, I think Loren would have been overwhelmed with the number of people who came to honor him and would have loved that the ceremony provided opportunities for both laughter and tears.

Being so involved with the details of the program has kept my grief temporarily at bay, and I'm stunned when Tina, whom I've known for over twenty years, comments, "Judy, I'm so glad you're not wearing black."

I'm wearing a simple linen dress that Loren bought for me, which matches my pale blue eyes. I never got to wear this dress with him, so I wanted him to see me in it at the service. When Loren gave it to me, he said, "I asked the salesgirl what dress would be good for springtime in Paris." I always marveled at his ability to buy clothes for me that made me feel beautiful and special. *Who will make me feel special now?*

The energy of the memorial service, especially the wonderful eulogies, carries me through this difficult day. My favorite speaker is Loren's fraternity brother Neil, who, after lumbering down the long aisle to the pulpit, says, "I'm listening to all the talks about Loren's great work in the field of psychiatry, his sensitivity to others, and his famous resignation from the American Psychiatric Association. But to me he was just 'Mo.' We got drunk together, had lots of fun, and thank god he was smart because he single-handedly maintained the necessary grade point average in our fraternity house while the jocks were screwing around."

Several weeks before the memorial service, my wonderful friend Sue had told me she was coming to San Diego to attend. Some innate wisdom had prompted me to ask her not to come to the service but instead to visit the week after, when everyone is gone and I'm alone. At a time when my soul was operating on low emotional batteries, one apparently had the necessary energy surge to make me remember that after a party the hostess becomes depressed — that after the memorial service and accompanying festivities end I will be alone to face a future without Loren.

Consequently, the week after the memorial service I feel grateful for Sue's support as I meet her at the airport. She has on a mint green sweat suit, her blonde hair falling naturally on her slightly freckled face. We hug and cry, but speak no words as they would serve no purpose. *How lucky I am to have such a friend, who knows that the depth of my sorrow is beyond words.*

With another person in the house, life returns to some normalcy. We know each other's habits and have shared many rituals over the years, such as going to the beach. When we lived in Maryland, prior to my marriage to Loren, we would get up at 5:00 a.m., jump in my bright orange Karmann Ghia convertible, put the top down, and make the two-hour drive to Rehoboth Beach. There we would sunbathe, turning over every twenty minutes, as if on a rotisserie spit until we were crisp, and eat donuts, French fries, and pizza, over the course of the day.

Here in San Diego we also go to the beach, this time in my sensible, old-lady silver-gray Honda Accord, bringing celery sticks to munch on. And we actually laugh, something I thought I would never experience again. In between trips to the beach, I talk to Sue about my financial concerns. She gets out a piece of yellow lined legal paper, on which she puts my expenses and my income, showing me that I don't have to worry about money.

After Sue leaves, I confront my financial concerns anyway. Loren left no will. We have a trust, all of which automatically comes to me, as the sole trustee. In my haze of grief, I somehow realize that it will be financially advantageous to me if Loren's two 401K accounts are rolled over into my own IRA account. *Is it okay to think of such mundane yet important things during the period of initial grief?*

Handling the 401K rollover turns out to be another gargantuan bureaucratic challenge, one worthy of the illogic expressed in *Alice in Wonderland*:

> *If I had a world of my own, everything would be nonsense. Nothing would be what it is, because everything would be what it isn't. And contrary wise, what is, it wouldn't be. And what it wouldn't be, it would. You see?*

When I call the firm in charge of the 401K to explain my situation, the voice at the other end of the telephone line says, "Can't do that. The beneficiary is the trust."

"But I am the trust," I answer with certainty, knowing my logic is correct.

It seems that what is isn't and what isn't is. But I refuse to lose sight of my goal, moving up the chain of supervisors until someone tells me I have to talk to the person in charge of the retirement plan from my husband's place of work.

"Fine," I say, my voice strong and stubborn, "just tell me whom to contact."

I make an appointment with this person, Sharon, who in my imagination wears a dark black, shapeless dress, a pointed black hat, has missing front teeth, carries a broomstick, and has a heart of ice—a witch who holds my financial future in her hands. I angrily pour my heart out to her, emphasizing the logic of my position. She sits quietly behind her desk and listens, then unexpectedly says, in a very unwitchlike way, "Of course I'll sign off on this. The same thing happened to me seven years ago when my husband died."

Again I experience the warmth of kindness, unexpected and welcome like the first crocus of the season.

Since Loren was retired from the military I have to inform the Public Health Service of his death and get a new military identification card as my status has changed from "dependent" to "widow." "Go to the nearest base, take a new picture, cut the old one up, and send it to our office," a faceless bureaucrat explains. The symbolism of cutting Loren's identification card with his photo into small pieces is too painful, another death.

I go to the nearest base, sit down for my picture, and start to cry. I explain to the photographer, a large-breasted African American woman, that I have to cut up Loren's identification card and send it back. She finishes taking the picture and says, "Don't worry, I'll send a letter to the main office saying I cut up the card. In the meantime I need to cut a tiny piece off the end so it cannot be used again, but you can keep it."

This kindness feels like a warm angora throw placed gently over my body. I put Loren's identification card in my wallet, feeling like I have been spared a small part of him.

As time goes on, I gradually learn how to accept more warmth and support from strangers, friends, family, and even neighbors I didn't know before. Although we had been living in the same residential neighborhood in San Diego for eight years before Loren's death, we had no close contact with neighbors, but after Loren's death one of my neighbors, who always identifies himself as "Steve, your neighbor to the left," says, "I know you're not the kind of person who likes to ask for help, but you are going to have to do that now." *I thought I left adolescence and overprotective parents behind! I know my husband died, but I can take care of myself.*

Although I initially dismiss the suggestion by this tall, bald man who looks like an ex-Marine, his statement stays with me, and indeed I end up asking for help with my computer, my phone line, and other tasks that Loren would have done. Other neighbors also help. When I take a trip and don't inform them, they yell at me because they worry. If they see someone coming into my house and they have not seen me, they call to check up on me. It has taken time and introspection to understand that they are not intruding in my life but simply being kind.

The warmth of kindness is the salve that makes the sting of death bearable, barely. There is no substitute, no "Sweet'n Low" or "Splenda" to replace the real thing. The grief does not disappear, but the shared burden makes it feel lighter and less overwhelming. The light rekindled by small kindnesses allows me to look through a tiny window and catch a glimpse of a possible future that might be filled with laughter, fun, and travel.

# 4

# The Widow's Mantra

"I AM RARELY ALONE BUT OFTEN LONELY" HAS BECOME MY WIDOW'S MANTRA. I'M surrounded by friends yet long for that part of me conspicuous by its absence. No one can fill the void left by Loren.

How different my mantra is from the one my mother used when she became a widow at age seventy-eight: "I'm always alone but never lonely." I imagine my mother in her favorite Bill Blass dress, black wool with pink silk lining and flared skirt, prancing around her apartment as if the world had not changed irrevocably for her. Every time I called, like the predictable chimes of the cuckoo clock she repeated those words. Then it seemed like she was speaking a foreign language. I couldn't identify with her situation since when my father died I had a husband whom I adored and a life full of fun and excitement. I thought I might understand her perspective better when I became a widow, but my feelings are different.

Living alone has always required a big adjustment for me, and now an even greater one since Loren and I were so compatible and close. The first time I lived alone I was twenty-eight. Before that I had lived at home until I was seventeen, in college dorms until age twenty-one, got married two weeks after college graduation, then divorced after seven years of marriage. I remember both the exhilaration and despair of the initial days after my divorce at twenty-eight, when at first I felt like a hang glider jumping off the crest of a mountain. I glided through the new region of freedom with elation—the wind in my hair, the sun in my face, money in my hand. I went to the most expensive clothing store and bought new outfits for my new lifestyle—hot pants suits, short dresses with plunging necklines, long dresses with slits up the side, bell-bottoms with matching tops. It felt great to develop my own style and spend my own money since previously I had given my husband my paycheck and received an allowance too meager for extravagant purchases.

Then during the despair phase I confronted intermittent storms and the possibility of a crash landing. The first storm, or challenge, was figuring out how to eat alone. At first, I simply avoided being home alone at dinnertime, staying out at malls, an unhappy wanderer amidst all the glitz, only returning home when there were no more shops to browse in. I know I can eat alone, I would affirm to myself. For several weeks, I set a formal table for one, with nice silver, sparkling crystal, bone china, flower napkin, and matching tablecloth. I had an appetizer, a main course, and a dessert. But I won the contest for speed eating, finishing in fifteen minutes to avoid facing the full implications of the ordeal.

The second storm, or challenge, after the divorce was learning to manage money. I had not been included in the bill paying since we had been the poster couple for a middle-class marriage, in which the wife cooked while the husband made all the monetary decisions. After the divorce, I had to think about my financial future for the first time. I wrote out a budget, crossed all my appendages, and hoped for the best. I was surprised to find out that I was good at managing money.

During the years of living alone, after the initial exhilaration and the intermittent challenges, things evened out. I was a free woman, excited and curious about how my life would develop. I went on dates—with ugly men with good personalities, handsome men with bad personalities, this one too short, that one too fat, the other one too involved with playing mind games, and so on. I developed my "Mr. Potato Head" theory: If I could take what I enjoyed about each date and construct one person, I would have the perfect male. I treated my state of singleness as a slight fever; with the right combination of interventions I would get better, find an appropriate partner. And eventually I did. Loren was the perfect Mr. Potato Head. Not only was he handsome, fun loving, and exciting, he was honest and nonjudgmental, characteristics very important to me. While I felt constrained by my first husband in many areas, with Loren I felt free and supported to develop my own personality. Furthermore, we had both been divorced the same amount of time, a reality that added to our compatibility.

But being a widow is very different from being a divorcée. When you become a widow, there is no initial exhilaration about being free, only sadness. I chose to get divorced, I did not choose to be a widow! Even the word seems ominous, making me picture big ugly poisonous black widow spiders that kill their mates.

Now I'm a star in a rerun of a familiar movie, but the plot changed. I again face the issues of aloneness in managing finances, eating, traveling, and sleeping, and while I know I can conquer those difficulties again, this time I have little hope that anything will be enjoyable. I feel like the best of my life is in the past and no longer look forward to the future. Some days I can't even deal with the present. I become aware of this gradually as I resume different activities following Loren's death. One day I drive up to Los Angeles to help my stepdaughter move into her new home, and when I see the carpool lane I dissolve in tears. *Shit, I can't even go into the carpool lane.* I shout to Loren, "I have to drive in the regular lanes, and I'm stuck in traffic all because you died." This unforeseen occurrence, like stepping on a sharp piece of glass hidden under the sand on the beach, is a startling reminder of the insidious and ubiquitous issues surrounding aloneness that surface after a spouse dies.

Although there are no scary financial issues after Loren's death, there are heartbreaking financial surprises. For example, because I had developed budgeting skills after my divorce, when Loren and I joined households we maintained financial independence. But after I successfully transfer his monies to the trust and call the broker to tell him of Loren's death, I get unexpected news of Loren's efforts to protect my resources.

"Loren called me before you went to Germany," the broker says, his voice choked up by the news, "and asked me to maximize your income."

Unaware of this, I'm speechless. I'm torn between anger and sadness and can barely manage a "thanks" before hanging up in tears. *Loren is still my protector, even in death.*

As for eating alone, there were many times in our marriage when I couldn't join Loren for meals, such as when he traveled to meetings. I enjoyed those times alone, as they were opportunities to have foods he disliked. But eating alone because of a death is very different—like being confronted with a locked door at the bottom of a staircase and walking back up the stairs only to find the door at the top also locked—with no exit.

Dining alone after Loren's death was difficult because of all the special associations we had with eating rituals. After we started to live together, I loved sitting next to him at the old, oblong oak table in his house. His animated facial expression, like a kaleidoscope held up to the light, changed with the topic of conversation. His eyes twinkled when he laughed, his lips trembled when he was trying not to cry, and he rubbed a tiny spot on the side of his face if he was thinking. At the table, we talked, laughed, cried, solved problems, and also ate.

Loren did most of the cooking because he liked to cook, while I did the shopping, chopping, and cleanup, except on nights he came home late from meetings when I prepared meals. On those occasions, I surrounded myself with cut-out recipes and cookbooks and obsessed about what to prepare. Loren cooked as he lived—without specific rules. He prepared wonderful nightly meals, including champagne risotto, asparagus with hollandaise sauce, steak au poivre, without so much as a cheat sheet in front of him. It pissed me off that I was a slave to the written word.

We always listened to music when we ate. Whoever was not cooking chose the music for the dinner hour. Loren liked Mahler and Gershwin; I favored Elton John and Cat Stevens. I always sang along with Cat Stevens's "Hard Headed Woman":

> *I'm looking for a hard headed woman,*
> *One who will take me for myself,*
> *And if I find my hard headed woman,*
> *I won't need nobody else . . .*

"That song reminds me of you," Loren said one evening after we had known each other for a year. I understood immediately. I accepted him for himself and didn't try to change him.

Sometimes during food preparation, Loren would come up to me, arms outstretched in dance position, and we would fox-trot around the beige tiled floors like Ginger Rogers and Fred Astaire floating across a moonlit stage.

Many memorable and profound incidents occurred at the dinner table. After Loren was diagnosed with cancer, mealtimes became opportunities for reviewing treatment options. It was at the dinner table that Loren told me, referring to possible treatments, "I can't do nothing; I have to try." It was at the dinner table that I tried to stave off the hopelessness of the situation by using such clichés as "Where there's life there's hope." And it was at the dinner table that Loren opened up a Father's Day gift from his Buddhist son Hal—a stunning silk thangka portraying a Buddha in the midst of colorful flowers—along with a card that read: "Poppa, hang this on the wall, and if you look at it at the moment of your death you will have a good transition." In response, I wrapped my arms around Loren as tightly as possible in an attempt to shield us from the future.

Now I miss the ritual around meals. There is no planning the day's meals, no chatting, just eating out of necessity. I'm not only the shopper but also the cook, another position for which I did not apply. Television makes noise and gives the semblance of company, but how many reruns of *Law and Order* can I watch?

I read somewhere that changing the usual place where you once ate with loved ones allows you to create new routines. I think of hermit crabs in the Caribbean that shed their old shells to find new ones. I try eating breakfast in another room, where the morning sunshine filters in, and the yellow, orange, and red gerbera daisies that I always keep in a yellow vase on the white Sarineen table add to the cheeriness. I read the newspaper, intentionally prolonging the meal.

Dinner parties present the next challenge. When Loren was alive, friends came for dinner at least once a week, filling our home with warmth and laughter. We loved opening our home to friends and took pride in the postmodern décor we had assembled over the years. My specialty was to set the table, with splashes of color everywhere: bright placemats on top of which sat white dinner plates and colorful salad plates; contrasting napkins; and polka-dot wine glasses. Before the company arrived, I always took Loren's hand and led him into the dining room, like an artist showing my finished canvas.

"Babe, that looks great," he would invariably say. I would return the compliment after tasting whatever he was preparing for the evening's meal.

Now the house feels empty and cold without dinner parties, and I am not sure how to fill the vacuum. I remind myself that I know how to cook and invite Connie and Roy over for dinner, which feels normal. But then I am confused about where to sit. *Do I sit in "my" place or do I sit in "Loren's" place? Where is my place now that I am a widow?* I know it is totally inappropriate to do a tableside coin toss to decide.

"Judy, it's okay to sit at the head of the table," Connie says, noticing my indecision.

I take the seat at the head of the table, but I feel like it is a betrayal of Loren. *Perhaps if I leave his seat empty he will magically appear.* I am reminded of the ritual during the Passover Seder of putting an extra glass of wine on the table for the prophet Elijah and leaving the door open so he can enter.

But even after the successful dinner party ends my uneasiness remains. *Will I ever find an emotional easy chair, where I can sit with happiness and confidence?*

Next I work on overcoming the emptiness and unease I feel while dining out alone. I invent a formula to help—a large amount of bravery and a touch of arrogance. In Venice, I walk into a small restaurant, crowded with couples, and say to the waiter, looking him straight in the eye, *"Uno, per favore."* My stomach churns with anxiety as I take a seat and stare down diners who look at me with pity. "How could you leave me? I am such a wonderful person, and we had such good times!" I silently fume at Loren before earning my widow's badge. After a few minutes, though, I am able to focus on ordering a dinner I ultimately enjoy.

Another major challenge to confront is traveling alone. Loren and I loved to venture to far-off places. He was the travel agent in the family, charming and chatting up those in charge until he got what he wanted, either an upgrade or a free trip. We traveled to Paris, Italy, New Zealand, Australia, even Lapland, where we stepped into a sauna without clothes, saw another nude couple, and chatted with them as if we sat with nude people every day.

There were so many places he promised to take me but never did, such as Russia, my father's homeland, Alaska to see nature, and Africa for a safari. I wonder if I will ever have the courage to go to these exotic places alone. *If I go on a group trip, will I still feel lonely?*

Three months after Loren dies I have to arrange my own travel to attend a meeting in Germany in his honor. I call the airlines to get an upgrade on this trip but can't chat up the woman at the other end of the phone and not only can I not get an upgrade, I can't even get a ticket for the dates that I need. My shoulders ache, my heart beats fast, my hands shake with frustration. *I wonder if there is such a thing as upgrade rage?* I finally tell the reservation person that my husband usually does the travel arrangements, that this is my first time as a widow doing it. *Since he died, it is difficult for him to get a line through to you.* I feel like I won an aging beauty contest; there is a big black sash across my breasts but instead of "Mrs. America" it says "Widow"—another role for which I did not apply.

I am also frustrated by single supplements on tours. *Why am I being punished because my husband died? Why should I have to pay more than some other woman who may not even like the man she is traveling with?* Sometimes I think I'll just take along one of those huge plastic dummies people use for carpool lanes, so I can get the regular rate and not feel like I'm traveling alone.

Then there is the challenge of sleeping alone. With Loren I learned the yumminess of skin-to-skin sleeping, with no pajamas or elegant negligee, and how to sleep joined together like spoons. Loren called me his "alter skin" because of the way we fit together. Every night throughout our marriage Loren, his front to my back and arm around me, would pull me close, and I would feel the soft head of his penis against my body and fall asleep feeling protected.

When my father died, Loren held me very close all through the night, as if holding me tightly would prevent me from feeling the sadness of death. But now Loren, the person who helped me deal with the first death of someone important to me, is not around to help me cope with his own death.

The night before Loren's first treatment in Germany he held me and said, "This is it, sweetums," as we silently shared our hopes and fears through our skins. That was the last time we snuggled—no more skin-to-skin, no more feeling protected in bed, no more hearing him call me sweetums.

I still sleep on my side of the bed, as if sleeping on his would be disrespectful or, worse, force me to acknowledge that he is not there. Seventeen months after Loren dies I have a dream about the agony of such an acknowledgment. In the dream, I wake up and realize that Loren is not on his side of the bed. I run my hand over the place to verify its emptiness. I decide he went to the bathroom and wait for him to return. He does not. "Oh, he's not in the bathroom. That's right, he's dead," I say out loud.

At that moment I accept his death more resolutely and realize that nothing I do can change it. My Ms. Fix-It mode will not help. The memorial service was perfect but still did not bring him back. I placed the ashes just as he wished, but he is not here.

As I continue adjusting to being dependent on myself to meet my needs, my widow's résumé expands from secretary of death and supervisor of ashes to include cook, travel agent, music director, decision maker, and driver. In the midst of such adjustments, I try to give myself permission to enjoy some of the positive aspects of being alone. For instance, when Loren was alive, we had frequent arguments about computer use as we shared one computer. Now no one tells me to get off the computer.

I was never a sloppy person and always cleaned papers off surfaces, and I expected the same of Loren, who sometimes did and other times did not. Now I leave my things anywhere and don't have to straighten up.

Loren and I were always cognizant of each other's schedules and tried to eat dinners together. I was flexible and would willingly change my plans to meet his more rigid schedule, although at times that got annoying. Now I come and go as I please without regard to anyone else's schedule. I loved Woody Allen films but had trouble getting Loren to go to first showings of the latest ones. Born and raised in California, Loren never appreciated his humor. I once convinced Loren to watch *Annie Hall* with me, positive that he would change his opinion, but he barely laughed. Now I see Woody Allen films when they first come to the theater.

Loren hated pizza, whereas I always thought of it as one of the food groups, a dietary necessity. So I either had pizza when he was away or while in a restaurant. Now I eat pizza at least once a week.

I try to adjust to my new roles and enjoy these freedoms I've found as I move through this intense process of coping with aloneness. Of course, I'd give them up in a minute if I could see Loren.

# 5

# Braving a Bereavement Group

*If you have formed a circle to go into,*
*Go into it yourself and see how you would do.*
— *William Blake*

"Why would I join a bereavement group?" I whine, incensed, into the telephone while talking to my best friend Sue. "I don't want to be a member of a club that would have me as a member," I continue, paraphrasing Groucho Marx's famous line. My poor attempt at humor doesn't make Sue laugh. "Will it make the pain go away? Will it bring Loren back?" I shout, my anger and tears making the words barely intelligible.

"No," Sue says, her gentle voice a salve to my pain. "It will not make the pain go away, but maybe it will help to talk with others whose spouses have died. You don't have to do this alone. Think about it."

I picture her freckled face, a half smile on her lips as she says this. Although I may not like what she says, I have learned over our twenty-nine years of friendship that she always expresses herself with love and concern, particularly when she speaks a truth I may not want to hear.

I immediately regret my outburst. "I'm so sorry," I say. "You don't deserve my anger."

"Don't worry," she says, unscathed by my eruption, "I don't take it personally. You've earned the right to be angry. Your best pal and husband just died. Think about it. Gotta go, love ya."

"Love you, too," I say and realize that I have not heard those words since Loren died.

I wish there were a number to call for assistance with the emotional breakdown sadness causes—an AAA for grief. But I know I have to find my own way in the mourning process, although I also need to learn how to accept the help of others now that Loren can no longer support me in grief. When my father died, not only did Loren hold me physically that first night but he cradled my emotions in the ensuing weeks. Then one day he said gently, "Judy, do you think you could spread your mourning around a little bit?" It was a Saturday morning, a time we liked to stay in bed late and make love. But because of my sadness we had not made love since my father had died. I looked in Loren's blue eyes trying to comprehend what he meant. Finally, I understood that he was telling me he could not be my sole support system during my time of grieving. So the next Monday I called a therapist, and from then on I found it very helpful to share my mourning in weekly therapy sessions. These sessions provided a place for me to slowly shed the weight of my grief. As a result, Loren and I were able to have fun instead of spending every minute focused on my sadness.

Now I remember what Loren said and wonder if I again need to spread my mourning around. I consider the possibility that I'm leaning on my friends too much and because they are too polite to tell me directly Sue suggested a bereavement group. The weekly sessions with my therapist Bev are useful, but it could be helpful to learn how others cope with the loss of a loved one. I remember the arguments I have used to convince clients to go to support groups. "It's good to find others with similar feelings," I would tell them. "You will feel relieved of some of your burden and learn of new solutions to your problems. You might even make new friends." I know all that, but I still don't want to go to a bereavement group.

I pick up one of my many books on grief to test my tolerance for therapeutic information, flip through it, then put it down, pick up another, flip through that too and put it down, unsure of what I'm looking for. Then I kick the whole stack of books so they tumble to the floor, an immature gesture that doesn't make me feel better. I want someone to tell me what to do. I'm tired of making all the decisions. Even the woman who provided the rules when I was growing up, my mother, can no longer show me the correct path to take. She has vascular dementia, can barely carry on a conversation, and while on good days she knows who I am she has no memory of Loren.

I review the conversation with Sue, wondering how I am going to tolerate someone else's grief when I can barely endure my own. I don't want to forget Loren, but I don't want to feel such intense pain either because Loren is on my mind every minute. The equation seems simple: Loren equals loss, which equals grief, which equals pain. Although not a mathematical equation, I wonder if changing one part of it will change the final result as well.

I picture a group of newly widowed men and women sitting in a circle with a huge box of Kleenex being passed to the person who is talking—a mourners' game of hot potato. I don't like the image, but I decide to brave a bereavement group in the hope it will help.

Wondering how to find such a group, I remember Robin mentioning that there was a list of them in the midst of the reading material she had brought to me. I locate the list surreptitiously stuck in the middle of one book, placed there so it seems more like an accident than a suggestion.

Now that I've identified a task to accomplish, I revert to my Ms. Fix-It mode. I call the ten groups on the list, find out when they meet, the cost, and the requirements. Some groups are for relatives of suicides only. Others are for parents whose children died. Forgetting my own grief for a moment, I think such survivors feel worse than I do. I learn that groups that charge a fee require an intake interview. As an experienced therapist myself, I know I will resent any group for which I have to pay when, in other circumstances, I could lead such a group. I finally choose a group that has weekly sessions and meets close to my home. Ease of getting there seems as good a criterion as any.

When the day for the session comes, I ponder what to wear to a grief group. *Do I have to wear all black? Do I bring my own tissues? What happens if I hate it and I'm called upon to speak?*

I feel so vulnerable. Bev knows me, so I trust her completely, but to open my heart to people I don't know feels like a tremendous risk, like having open-heart surgery with the possibility of unknown complications and even severe rejection. Nevertheless, I go to the meeting place, an apartment building for seniors. I have nothing against seniors, being one myself, but this seems like a bad omen. I'm afraid that I will find only old people who look depressed, deprived of any vim or vigor. Caught in a web of ambivalence, my right hand puts my car in reverse, while my right foot almost guns the gas. Finally I force myself to park and enter the building.

I crinkle up my nose as I smell Lysol, an odor I instantly associate with hospitals and nursing homes, sickness and death. *Are people dying here, or am I being overly dramatic?* Cautiously, I look around the reception area, where everything is perfect: there are shiny wood floors with no evidence that anyone walks on them, silver print wallpaper with no smudges, plastic-covered lobby furniture that blends in perfectly with the walls, smiles on all the faces of the people in the lobby. *I must have taken a wrong turn and ended up in the adult equivalent of Disney World.* The pain of my grief is for the moment eclipsed by a feeling of despair, but I stay, in the hope of obtaining some relief from grief.

I take the elevator to the twelfth floor and look into the appointed room. I'm early, and no one else is there yet. The chairs are in a circle, the usual arrangement for a psychotherapy group, although this is supposed to be just a support group. Small white Dixie cups filled with red-colored punch are lined up on a small bridge table, like soldiers in a row, and some cookies—the typical snack for either very young children or hospital patients.

I have that sinking feeling in my stomach, which often occurs when I'm conflicted about the right thing to do. I desperately want to leave, but I made a commitment to myself to try this. I stay. I choose a seat and keep my head down. *Perhaps if I don't see anyone they won't see me.* Suddenly I realize that is the magical thought of a two-year-old. A surge of feelings forces my head down even lower—dread about the group, fear that I will cry, fear that I won't cry, worry that I will be the youngest in the group and have nothing in common with anyone else, and an equal dread that I really do belong here.

I hear the shuffle of feet as others wander in and take a seat. I look up to see I have stepped backwards in time. Women who live in the 1950s surround me, indistinguishable in their washed-out mint green, faded fuchsia, and not quite baby blue polyester pants and matching tops, fingernails and toenails painted in variations of bright red, and hair teased to the limit. There is only one man in the group, with two hearing aids. Clearly I am the youngest one in this group. I am convinced that even if I need a support group this weird one is not for me. But I'm curious enough to stay.

"My name is Jack, and I am ninety-two years old," says the man in the group. "I just returned from a field trip to the beach. I sure wish my wife could've been with me." I look at this elderly man and realize how happy I would be if Loren had lived to be ninety-two, double hearing aids and all. I feel sad for him, being so alone.

"I lost my husband a couple of months ago," another group member says. *I always wondered about that phrase. If you lose a husband, can't you just find him again, even if you have to take out an advertisement in the paper? Here I go again, trying to use humor to relieve stress and anxiety.*

"My best friend, my companion, died last week," another woman sobs. "He was my pet for ten years, a miniature poodle named Anatole. I miss him so much."

I know it's very difficult when a pet dies. Earl, the adorable black lab that my stepdaughter and son-in-law acquired when they first met, died after seven years, which was traumatic for them. But how can this woman, in her baby blue polyester pantsuit talk about the death of her pet in the same room with men and women who are struggling with the death of a spouse? I clamp my mouth shut so I don't scream at the leaders.

Soon it's my turn, and I have to figure out the proper etiquette for introducing myself. "My husband died in July," I say. I don't cry. These are the only words I utter during the entire session. I stay until the end of it, but I know I will not return. The one good result is an offer of free journals for everyone—pretty spiral books with variations of green clouds on the cover. I drive back home to the safety of my sad nest, where I write a journal entry about the group:

> *I tried and failed. No. I didn't fail; the group failed me. It just wasn't a good fit. To hell with bereavement groups. I'll be as sad as I want, and eventually it will subside—or will it?*

For several weeks, I avoid thinking about bereavement groups, relying on my sessions with Bev to give me support. My friends are wonderful, but I know I have to try again, as Loren said, "to spread my mourning around" in order to decrease the burden on my friends.

One day I peruse the list again, deciding to rely on random association rather than logic to pick a group, like picking a horse at a racetrack. I discover a bereavement group that meets in the same small town where my therapist has her office and like the name of the sponsor of the group, "Hospice by the Sea," which reminds me of sailing.

I list the pros: it is near my therapist, and it meets at a convenient time. I'm feeling quite alone with my grief and would like to know how others are coping and what solutions they might have found. *Are there solutions to grief?* Although the group is part of a senior program, it is in a community center.

I review the cons: I don't want Loren to be dead, and I really don't want to talk about it. I hated the last bereavement group. I have a fear that if my grief lessens I will forget Loren. I tally the pros and cons and conclude that the pros outweigh the cons. Reality wins over denial, and I decide to try this new bereavement group.

I go to the community center Monday at 1:00 p.m., take a deep breath, throw my shoulders back, and gamely walk into the room. Immediately it feels better. An assortment of women sit around the rectangular table, no food, no cookies or bug juice, as we campers used to call that red liquid. And there is a small tasteful box of tissues in the center of the table. The woman who sits at the head of the table has soft gray hair, warm eyes, and a smile that invites me in. She wears lavender plaid slacks and a stylish top of some kind, no polyester, no bright red nails, and no bleached, excessively bouffant hair.

"My name is Sally," she says. "I'm the leader of this group. What's your name?" I tell her my name and sit down.

"This is a very safe place to be," Sally says, after she closes the door and takes her seat. "It's okay to cry. We talk about our experiences with death . . . and life."

When it is my turn to speak, I say, "My husband died two months ago of liver cancer," trying to hide the sorrow in my voice. The older grayish blonde woman sitting next to me touches my shoulder gently, nonintrusively. I turn slightly to my left, and we smile at each other. I see my smile reflected back to me from her gold-rimmed glasses and I know I am in the right place.

I learn that the group has eight women in different stages of grief — some whose husbands died years ago, and others whose husbands died more recently — all of whom receive support during the session. I am the youngest in this group and feel enfolded in their maternal caring. For the hour and a half that we are together, we become a closely knit sorority, protective of all our sisters. At the end of the session, we all participate in the closing ritual — hugging each other. At first I think this is weird, but receiving my first hug I realize how much I miss being touched. I decide to keep attending meetings of this bereavement group, which I find supportive.

At the beginning of all subsequent sessions, Sally asks, "What did you do for yourself this week?" The question always surprises me as I am so busy facing Loren's death and the attendant tasks that I don't think about myself. But Sally's question reminds me that it is okay to take care of myself as well as Loren — an important revelation for me. I find myself anticipating this weekly question, which gives me permission to focus more on my needs. As a result, I resume my monthly pedicure, allow myself some fun with my friends, and go back to work.

I'm attracted by the diversity of this group. There are women from all stages of life and all income levels with vastly different experiences. One woman never worked a day in her life and now doesn't know how to proceed. Another woman's husband had always taken care of everything, including the bills, and she knows nothing about finances. I feel needed when I can provide her with some pertinent information. There is one woman who seems more interested in consistently crying about her story than moving forward and yet another woman straight out of the West, with prairie skirts and lots of turquoise and silver jewelry, who reports talking to herself whenever she feels she is "boo hooing." Yet we share the powerful experience of death and the need to talk about it.

Sally's husband, who was much older than she, died several years ago. She clearly misses him and describes how hard it was for her after he died. Yet she now has a "male friend, " someone she cares about and with whom she can have some fun. I marvel at her ability to acknowledge her loss and yet move on. She represents the possibilities that are ahead of me. I wonder if I will ever be able to move forward and have a male friend.

The most amazing group member is Maria, a diminutive ninety-two-year-old Hispanic woman whose husband of sixty-eight years just died. Her short hair is still black, and her lovely face exhibits the scars of time. She dresses sedately, always in black, and wears lovely gold earrings, pins, and chains. "I discover that if I shop I forget about my husband for a few hours," she reports one week, throwing her shoulders back in a gesture of pride. The following weeks she reports on the various clothes she bought that are now hanging untouched in her closet because she will not wear them until her year of mourning is up. Then Maria describes how, despite the shopping, she cries most of the time and cannot stay alone in her apartment. We give her encouragement. It occurs to me that I have not been clothes shopping since Loren died, and I go to one of my favorite stores, Chico's, amazed that for those few hours I am totally focused on clothes and not Loren's death. I am equally surprised that I look good in so many of the things I try on. I buy them and don't feel the need to wait until the year of mourning is up to wear them.

I learn that everyone has their own way of coping, and there is no right or wrong way to mourn. I ponder my own way of calling friends, writing in my journal, traveling, and crying.

It is with this unusual group of women that I begin to share my own experiences of grieving. I report my adventures with the ashes, and we all laugh. I never thought I would laugh again let alone about events concerning Loren's ashes. I talk about my demented mother and how difficult it is to deal with her at this time when I am also coping with Loren's death. I share my intense love for Loren accompanied by my experiences of loss and feel that they understand.

Sometimes they express amazement at my ability to deal with bills, children, and work. This surprises me, but I welcome the acknowledgment of competence, something Loren used to provide.

Anne, the woman I had sat beside during my first visit, describes her persistence with a lawyer, and we cheer her on. I remember how Loren insisted that we see a lawyer to make sure everything was in order. Sybil, who came to San Diego to live with her daughter after the death of her husband, cries when she describes how much she misses her old life and friends. I realize how Loren provided constancy for me—I have enough money, and I don't have to move. I am grateful for his planning. Although my life has been turned upside down by Loren's death, it is still amazingly stable.

I'm surprised when I realize that I look forward to these weekly meetings. I never expected to find a sisterhood of such unusual women in a bereavement group. We are soldiers in the battle of life as we nudge one another forward. We laugh at each other's mistakes, make fun of the weaknesses, and take pride in our accomplishments. My major accomplishments are learning to laugh at myself and not feeling guilty for enjoying life. I am grateful to these women who support my grief, allow me to give some of my unspent caring and love to them, and remind me that I am a worthwhile person apart from Loren. The hole in my heart begins to heal a little bit. My grief doesn't go away and I still cry a lot, both by myself and with the group, but a slow change is occurring. The hermit crab is again trying to find a new, more comfortable shell. I reflect in my journal: "Everything seemed to be about endings . . . Now it seems to be about new beginnings although I still miss Loren so much."

After a year passes, the group begins to feel like an obstacle, keeping me from moving forward in my life, away from grief and mourning. I feel less needy and want to spend the time doing other activities—writing, working, traveling, or visiting friends, yet I can't predict when grief will suddenly overwhelm me. Grief seems like a capricious child. There are times when the child is invisible, and for those moments life feels free. Then unexpectedly this child appears from nowhere and continues to return no matter what, although perhaps less frequently as time goes by.

I tell the group I'm leaving. "Sally, this is my last day. I will stop by now and then to let you know I'm okay," I say with tears in my eyes as I give her a big hug.

"You're ready to move on, dear," she says. " You have a whole life ahead of you. Go out and live it." I have completed the credits of this course and now must go out and apply my knowledge. I have no idea how it will work out but am excited to try.

Sometimes, when I feel I need a hug, I go to the community center and talk to Sally for a few minutes. But I always leave before the group starts.

It is not my group anymore.

# 6

# Confronting His Clothes

*When from a long-distant past nothing subsists,*
*after the people are dead, after the things are broken and scattered,*
*still, alone, more fragile, but with more vitality, more unsubstantial, more persistent,*
*more faithful, the smell and taste of things remain poised a long time, like souls,*
*ready to remind us, waiting and hoping for their moment amid the ruins of all the rest;*
*and bear unfaltering, in the tiny and almost impalpable drop of their essence,*
*the vast structure of recollection.*

*—Marcel Proust*

"IT'S ANOTHER BEAUTIFUL DAY HERE IN SAN DIEGO, AMERICA'S FINEST CITY," booms the cheerful radio announcer in the background.

"No, it's not," I say out loud, "it's another sad day in San Diego." I'm circling in front of Loren's closet, a cat deciding whether or not to pounce. I take the challenge, jerk the doors open, and see Loren's clothes still there. For a few seconds Loren is alive even though it's been about two and a half months since he died. I feel as though a rush of heat is smothering me and am confused. For a second I think this is all a dream and he will soon return. I shake my head to try to rearrange my perceptions. Then I back away from the closet and close the doors. *What am I going to do with his clothes?*

It's a Saturday morning, a day that used to promise fun. But no longer. There is no Loren, no lovemaking, no talking. I have no plans and no place to go. A line from The Platters' song "Unchained Melody" goes through my mind: "Time goes by so slowly and time can do so much . . ." Right now time feels like an old lady barely able to move forward. *Or am I that old lady?*

I force myself to go outside and bring in the newspapers, but I still have trouble focusing. I've lost track of my favorite comic strip, *Doonesbury*. I don't care about *Cathy* anymore. We went through our single life together, but she's now married and I'm a widow. No identification there. I put the papers down on the kitchen counter and eat breakfast standing up—some fruit, cottage cheese, and tea. At least I've used up fifteen minutes of my day, which looms ahead of me like a long, treacherous ocean voyage.

I wander through the house and go back into the bedroom. I'm cold, even though the temperature is warm. I put on my old high school sweatshirt. It usually brings me comfort but not today.

"What do you need, Judy?" Loren would ask me when I said I didn't feel right.

"A hug," was my usual answer. But that's not possible now.

I call Sue, who always helps me gain my footing.

"Guess what I just did?" I say with no inflection in my voice. "I opened up Loren's closet, and his things are . . . " My voice is stopped by tears.

"They're still in the closet," Sue says, finishing my sentence. "It must be very hard looking at his clothes. Perhaps it's time to think about what you want to do with them," she adds, with no implication that I should act now. "But do it on your own schedule. I have a patient whose daughter died two years ago, and she still has not touched anything in the room."

"God," I scream into the phone, "two years! I hope I can do this before two years pass." But even as I scream into the phone I realize that, as with the dispersal of ashes, dispersal of clothing is a very personal process. I will do it my own way. There is no book of rules on how to proceed and no prize for speed.

After we hang up, I go back and stand in front of the closet, no longer a cat ready to pounce but a claustrophobic adult going into a dark cave for the first time. That unseen, powerful force confronts me as before. Again I'm overwhelmed. *How am I ever going to do this?*

I remember that when my father died my mother immediately emptied the closets and the drawers, called a charity to pick up his clothes, and within a day everything was gone. It was as if a tornado had swept through her apartment and removed all objects that would indicate to future archaeologists that another human being had lived there. But I can't do that. I don't want to do that.

"Get rid of his clothes quickly," some friends advised soon after Loren died. "It will help you let go." *Who wants to let go?* The truth is I want to hold on to Loren, or at least the memory of him. I had some of the happiest moments of my life with him. Why would I want to forget those?

Also, perhaps the more I put off getting rid of Loren's things — or "effects," as they are called by people who want to distance themselves from emotion — the longer I can pretend that Loren is away on one of his long lecture tours and will return in a couple of weeks. Or maybe it's just that the house feels empty enough without also having an empty closet and dresser staring me in the face as visual reminders of a void that can't be filled.

I remind myself that I managed the dispersal of the ashes, which seems even harder. Yet that was with friends who provided both support and levity to a weird situation. Now I am alone in the house trying to make decisions that I don't want to make. Since there is no manual, maybe I can use the child's nursery rhyme to make this decision: "Eenney, meenny, minny, mo, / Catch a tiger by the toe, / If he hollers let him go / My mother said to choose this one. / So out goes Y-O-U."

"I was talking to Karenlee," Loren said when we had a quiet moment at his seventieth birthday party, "and I was encouraging her to clean out the closets, get rid of Richard's things and move on. After all, he died two months ago." Loren made a gentle motion with his hand, ushering out the past. I looked over at Karenlee, dressed in her signature shade of lavender, this time a long flowing skirt and silk blouse, but with her face looking wan. I admired her for coming to the party despite her grief.

I never thought that just one year later I would be facing the same decisions, the same amount of time after Loren died. It sounded right when Loren told Karenlee to move on, yet I'm not sure I want to "move on" and have fun with others. *Because of what he said, maybe I have his permission to do it. Sounds rational, but how can I make such serious decisions without him? Maybe the emperor does have clothes after all, and Loren will come back.* The soothing sameness, timeless wisdom, and magical beliefs of nursery rhymes and children's stories give me a much-needed sense of control in the face of this unfathomable occurrence called death.

After standing in front of the closet for about ten minutes while these thoughts go through my head, I realize I'm not ready to act. I wander into Loren's office to the poster I made for him and displayed at his seventieth birthday. I read out loud the message by Lord Byron about Don Juan that I put on it, incorporating Loren's name: "There is something awfully swell about a man as passionate lunatic fun-loving hedonistic and noble as [Loren Mosher]. . . . a true voluptuary will never abandon his mind to the grossness of reality. And that's the essence of the free spirit—reality never gets in his way. So on that note we invite you to delight in a little make-believe. It's what fashion does best."

The quotation was perfect for my fun-loving Loren, who loved fashion and delighted in the make-believe inspired by clothes. I enjoyed watching his studied dressing process, a lovely, predictable ballet: first, he carefully chose slacks or a suit; next, he selected a coordinated shirt, which he would hold to the light to make sure it matched; finally, he looked at his fifty plus ties—which he used as an artist does when putting finishing touches on a painting—chose several, narrowed the choice down to two, then sought out my opinion. He really cared about the way he presented himself and often looked like an ad for men's clothing.

"Loren is sort of a dandy. He's like a girl the way he loves clothes and jewelry, isn't he, Judy?" my mother once said with that way she had of making a simple observation into a nasty comment.

"Mom, he likes clothes. What's the big deal?" I answered in an angry tone, like a lioness protecting the king of the pride. She didn't understand that I loved the care and joy Loren showed when getting dressed, which had nothing to do with money spent but was instead an expression of his love of life that was contagious to those around him. When Loren wore his tuxedo with the crazy Nicole Miller tie and cummerbund that had all kinds of gambling icons on it to the Metropolitan Opera House, people would often come up to him and comment, always with a smile on their faces. He relished such moments, confirmation of his delight with life.

Loren was not always the fashion plate he was in later years, but his clothes always made a statement. When he was younger, he once wore old, worn-out jeans, a T-shirt, and a Confederate cap when he gave an important professional lecture about the dangers of psychiatric medications and the significance of just being with the patient.

"Loren," I said in frustration, "if you're going to give a provocative lecture, at least dress in a conservative pin-striped suit so people won't stop listening before you even begin."

"You're right," he said, a mischievous smile forming on his lips that reflected his rebellious nature.

Loren said he hated to shop, but what he meant was he didn't like to browse clothing. He made quick decisions. It only took him ten minutes to pick out and order a stunning dark pin-striped suit from a Brioni shop in Venice, annoying me because I love to linger over each piece of clothing. In Paris, as I obsessed about a Pucci shirt and tiny black camisole top Loren quickly picked out a light blue linen jacket, which matched his eyes. Then he encouraged me to buy the outfit, commenting on how sexy the camisole top was. He loved to see me in "sexy clothing," while I, always shy, would cover up. I did buy the outfit, however, and wore it that evening to the Paris Opera House, where we saw an exquisite ballet performance of *Les Sylphides*. The love and enjoyment in his eyes when he looked at me that night wiped away any doubts I had about my purchases.

Loren particularly loved buying ties such as the lovely green, swirled hand-painted one that we purchased in a paper shop in Florence and the Missoni one in variegated shades of blue and gray that I bought for him as I wandered the Lido in Venice while he was giving lectures on how to deal with people who hear voices. I enjoyed listening to Loren's lectures, but sometimes I would instead roam the streets and shops, surprising him with a special gift.

Once roused from my reverie, I realize that each piece of clothing in Loren's closet represents an experience we shared together. *If I get rid of the clothing, will the memories disappear as well?* I hesitate, afraid to take the risk. I tell myself I'm waiting for the children to come and look again to see if they want anything else, but I know I'm just not ready to face this issue.

When the children came to the memorial service, I felt foolish asking them to look through their dad's clothes to see if there was anything they wanted. They seemed pleased with the prospect, however. After trying on a jacket and wondering if she could have it altered to fit her, Missy settled on a white T-shirt "that smelled like Dad" to keep in her drawer, as well as a black Borsalino hat. Loren always wore hats despite the fashion of the moment: panama hats in summer, and brown, blue, or navy Borsalino hats in winter. I used to tease him, telling him he looked like a rabbi when he wore a black hat and black coat. *No more teasing. Another piece of the loss.*

After poking through the closet, Tim had tried on some shirts, but they were all too small. "It all comes down to stuff," he said with sadness in his voice.

"I guess that's right," I replied, echoing the sadness, "but it can help to have something concrete as a reminder." Although painful, for me it had been helpful to have objects around the house that remind me of Loren and reaffirm the life we had together.

"I'll just take some of these small boxes from the dresser to remind me of Dad," he finally said, removing a few small jewelry boxes that had been on Loren's dresser since I had met him thirty years before. I was hopeful that Tim would one day look at those tokens of Loren and smile at the memories they brought.

On this long Saturday, after recalling these memories, I suddenly decide to face Loren's clothing, as if being forced to finally deal with an infection that one would rather ignore. In addition, I realize that since Loren no longer needs a closet I can expand my own closet space. I'm embarrassed by the concern for my own needs, and then a very slight smile forms as yet another memory surfaces.

"Judy," Loren would say whenever we entered a hotel room on our travels, "you're a space-occupying lesion. Is there no space for me?"

"What do you mean?" I would ask, my eyes wide with an expression of innocence.

"Look around the room and see if there is one place where you have not put any of your things," he would counter. And I would look around the room and laugh because, sure enough, every surface had something of mine on it, whether it was the bed with my coat, the desk with my purse, or the chair with my backpack.

I'm getting ready to face the closet but want to wash my hands first, since it feels like a sacred task. I go into the bathroom and realize with a start that many of my cosmetics and lotions are already on his side of the sink. *How did that happen? I don't remember doing that. Space-occupying lesion?* When we first moved into this house with double sinks, we laughed as we brushed our teeth in tandem, a totally new activity of togetherness. Now I have more space on the sink. *Is this what "moving on" means? Filling up spaces that are left vacant by his death? Yet I did it without thinking, without guilt. Perhaps letting go and moving on happen by themselves?*

I sit on the beige-carpeted floor and face one piece of clothing at a time: the tuxedo Loren wore to the Metropolitan Opera House, hand sewn by Sylvio, a tailor in Verona with whom we always had several glasses of Custoza wine as he was taking Loren's measurements; the Saville Row tuxedo shirt Loren bought and then wore to Covent Gardens when we saw *Romeo and Juliet*; a chic charcoal gray pin-striped shirt I just bought him last Valentine's Day that, along with a suit, light tie, and black hat, made him look like a roguish Al Capone.

Valentine's Day feels like a lifetime ago, and yet it feels like yesterday. The memories, like pieces of fabric left in the sun for several months, are both faded and unchanged, depending on which part I see.

Continuing to sort through clothing, I pick up a bright blue silk sports jacket that matched Loren's eyes, one I bought for him several Christmases ago. I finger the gold Canali jacket purchased in Venice, which looked perfect on Loren, even though I had to iron it every time he wore it. Wherever we traveled, clothing displayed in shop windows provided familiar landmarks I remembered to find my way back to hotels, like Hansel and Gretel using breadcrumbs they had dropped to find their way home. It's a painful process, like slowly pulling a Band-Aid off a cut. I'm not the quick-pull type eager to get the pain over with quickly.

I decide I want to keep some of Loren's jackets to wear. *Perhaps just seeing them in the closet will help bridge me to my own travels.* I remember when my father died I kept his raw silk jacket in the closet, periodically looking at it, trying it on, smiling, and putting it back on the hanger, until I finally gave it away after he had been dead for about ten years. It was comforting to touch it and think about my dad, letting it help with the transition.

I put aside two of Loren's special jackets, the gold Canali from Venice and the light blue one from Paris. I keep some of his T-shirts to use as nightshirts, hopeful that wearing them will bring me closer to Loren at night, when the emptiness is most oppressive.

I feel glum while reporting to Karenlee at dinner, "Well, I faced Loren's clothes, but I don't know what to do with some things." I continue, picking at my food, "It seems so final to get rid of them, but I don't want them either."

"Designate one drawer in Loren's dresser as a place for the things you don't want to give away but don't want to see all the time," she suggests.

I go home that night and choose the middle drawer in his, now my, dresser, because it is unlikely that I will pull it open and be surprised to find Loren's things in it. I pick out some items and put them in the drawer: the special Grateful Dead T-shirt with the motto "Keep on truckin'" that Loren, a Deadhead, wore to all the concerts; a T-shirt from a club at Bass Lake, where he worked when he was sixteen and took me last year; and some turtlenecks I bought for him. I think I may wear some of these things and realize at the same time that I probably won't. Loren looked great in them, but they're not my kind of shirts.

"Okay, Suz, I finished sorting them," I report with relief during our next phone call. "Now what do I do with them? They represent so many memories."

"How about giving them to a local charity?" she suggests, being logical as usual.

"Are you kidding?" I screech into the phone. "I can't just put them in a plastic bag and give them to the local Goodwill. Aside from possibly freaking out if I saw them on some street person, I feel as though they deserve better."

"Judy," she says, her voice calm, "these are things, not people."

"I know, but I feel as if I will be throwing Loren away if I just discard the clothes. I realize Loren is already dead and he won't mind. But I just want to be respectful and practical at the same time," I answer.

"Well, you got through the first step, you'll figure this out, too," she says, a loyal cheerleader.

I hang up the phone and pull out the phone book. I'm on a mission. *But what do I look under? Stores that receive precious clothing filled with memories?* I look up thrift stores: Salvation Army, Goodwill Industries, Amvets. Although I donate to these organizations, they don't seem right for the possessions of a psychiatrist noted in his field. Loren's clothes feel alive to me, like a beating heart. As with an organ transplant, it seems important to me for the clothes to end up with someone who really needs them and will understand their value. I then turn to consignment shops, finding several that say "designer clothing." I'm embarrassed to be selling these clothes. It's not for the money; my logic is that by selling them to an elite shop, as opposed to disposing of them, I am honoring Loren and preserving his integrity. Or is it a reflection of my need for dignity? I decide to go to a shop that buys elegant clothes and see if they will buy these things worn by my elegant husband. I pick a shop in La Jolla, the expensive part of town, determined to arrange the best for Loren, even in death.

I feel as though I'm going on an important college interview that will change the course of my life. Like college acceptance, which foreshadows moving on from home, relinquishing Loren's clothes is also a step away from the past toward a new, unknown future. I shower, put on nice black slacks and a shirt, and makeup, something I have not done in a while.

I drive to the shop and find a parking space out front. *Thanks, Loren. I take that as a sign that you approve of what I am doing.*

I enter the shop, which smells like spring. The mirrors on the wall reflect racks of neat and attractive women's clothing. I idly check the labels of some items: a suit by Chanel, a black leather jacket by Dolce and Gabbana, a gorgeous white sweater by Versace, and a lovely plum-colored pantsuit by Tahari. All seem to be designer names and priced accordingly.

I approach the saleswoman, who looks lovely in a red designer suit. "Do you sell men's clothes?" I ask, not sure if I want the answer to be yes or no.

"Yes," she answers, "let me get Claude."

Claude appears, elegantly dressed in a stunning light gray suit, pale blue shirt, and Missoni tie. "I understand zat you want to zee the men's clothes," he says with a slight accent.

"Oh no, I'm sorry," I say, as we shake hands. "I have some clothes I would like to sell. They're in the trunk of my car."

We go to the car and carry in all the clothes and shoes. Claude picks up each item of clothing, looks inside at the seams and outside at the cloth, then comments, "Yes, I can szell that" or "No, I cannot." I feel like I'm in a gym and the captains are picking team members. Every article of clothing is silently screaming, "Pick me, pick me." *Again I am giving life to these lifeless items.* Every yes makes me feel as joyful as I can at this time, and every no increases already intense feelings of loss. And yet every yes also takes another piece of Loren from me. Such are the inconsistent emotions of grief.

I feel like I am letting Loren down, but I cannot figure out how. Finally, Claude tells me that he can buy them for $800, if that price is agreeable to me.

"Okay," I say, as I stand there stunned by the mention of money. I know they are good clothes, but I feel guilty for taking that amount of money, as if caught with my hand in the cookie jar. I want to pay tribute to Loren and have his clothes in this chic store, but I don't want to make a profit so I decide I will not use the money for my own enjoyment but donate the money to a fund in Loren's name that will support projects perpetuating his work. I'm also angry that the other clothes have not been picked. *Are they not good enough for this place?* Eventually, I take them to a less pricey consignment shop, say good-bye to them, and ask the woman to sell them. Although I won't receive much money for them, I can honor Loren by donating that money as well.

In my closet I keep the two jackets of Loren's and one bright blue shirt. Several times a week I put on one of the jackets or the shirt, look in the mirror, then take it off. I realize they are not right, even though the jackets, now altered, fit perfectly and look good, too. The seamstress who modified them knew Loren and thought it was a great idea, and at the time I did also. Now the idea strikes me as one of those impulsive acts that you later question — like spontaneously dying your hair one day then looking in the mirror and wondering, "Why did I do this? It's not really me."

Ironically, I had the clothes altered because I thought wearing them would enable me to feel closer to Loren, but the opposite happens. Every time I put on the jackets I am reminded once again that he's not here. Putting on the clothes, being reminded of Loren, and then taking them off, is like picking at a slowly forming scab. I don't know how long it will take for the scab to turn into a scar. Sometimes it seems like it will never happen, and at other times I feel hopeful.

# 7

# Daring to Believe

*The purpose of life, after all, is to live it, to taste experience to the utmost,*
*to reach out eagerly and without fear for newer and richer experiences.*

—*Eleanor Roosevelt*

AFTER LOREN DIES, MY STRUGGLE TO UNDERSTAND THE PURPOSE OF DEATH HAS more urgency. In my mind, I believe that making sense of Loren's death and being able to envision where he is now will be the magic wand that lessens my grief. When he traveled, I could picture where he was at any given time, and although I missed him I was comforted by that knowledge. Now, in addition to the emptiness in the house and in my heart, there is a void in my mind. *If I can just place him somewhere, visualize where he is . . .*

The demons of death kept me up many nights when I was young. I could not picture nothingness; nor could I understand how the world would go on without me. My father quelled my nightly fears until those demons subsided. And after years of therapy I understood that part of my fear was a result of having a narcissistic mother. We were so connected, my seven-year-old mind was convinced that if I died she would die as well. When my father died, I again focused on death. Although I was a grown woman with a wonderful husband, I intensely felt the loss of my childhood protector and tried to fill the void. As my mother and I were approaching the funeral home, I found a penny on the sidewalk and remarked, "Look, Mom, Dad is sending us pennies from heaven." Since then my father's protection and love lived on through every coin I found, which made me picture my father throwing pennies to me from heaven, an image to fill my emptiness.

I recall how, about ten years ago, Loren said, sorrowfully, "Bruce is not going to last long," as we drove away from a visit with his longtime friend. "The diagnosis of esophageal cancer is a death sentence."

"What do you think happens after death?" I asked Loren. I looked around the crowded California freeway, and a giggle escaped my lips.

"What's so funny?" he asked, his irritation with my levity evident.

"Sorry, I just thought that anyone who looks at us riding in this snappy red convertible would be appalled to hear our discussion. Anyway, what do you think happens after death?" I asked again.

"Well," he said, "I asked Bruce the same question. He believes that when you're dead you're dead."

I felt the dreaded demons of death closing in, even as the trite words from the Peggy Lee song "Is That All There Is?" slipped into my mind. Still, I persisted. "But what do *you* think?"

Loren's answer did little to calm my uneasiness. The picture of my father rotting in the ground was horrifying, and I much preferred the image of him throwing pennies from heaven.

Even though rituals of the Jewish religion had helped ease my grief after my father died, they had never provided me with a coherent, peaceful vision or understanding of death. When I witnessed Loren's peaceful crossing to the other side, I became less frightened but more confused.

The continuous question I ask myself is, "Where is Loren?" Or, more existentially, "Is he at all?" Sometimes I experience the usual post-death sensations of feeling his presence in the bedroom. Or I feel him snuggling in, causing a fleeting moment of safety. I tell him I love him, discuss decisions and events, and yell at him for leaving me. I ask him questions and imagine answers that don't exist. Although these experiences keep Loren alive for me, none speaks directly to my question about death.

One day Loren's son Hal gives me a book about the Tibetan tradition of death. I find the Buddhist belief that death is an extension of life a comforting thought and consistent with my experience of Loren's transition. But my need to know where Loren is persists.

In an effort to bring increased calm to my life, and broach the topic of death with my supportive acupuncturist Laurie, also a Buddhist, I make my acupuncture appointments closer together. One afternoon I'm lying on the table as Laurie sticks needles in the various points so my qi moves around and helps me through these difficult months. Standing there with her long dark blonde hair, fair skin, and tall frame, surveying all the points like a satisfied artist, she says, "Judy, I know a terrific medium, someone who can commune with the dead." *Are you nuts? I feel weird enough lying on this table with needles sticking out of me.*

"Not yet," I say, afraid that even the slightest movement of my lips will cause the needles to fall out. "It's too soon, and I feel too raw." My instinct tells me that no matter how such an experience turned out I'm not ready to face even the possibility of communing with the dead. Yet as the year passes, and I let go of ashes, clothes, and dreams but not memories and yearnings, the idea appeals to me. I crave some kind of knowledge about or contact with Loren, for comfort or closure.

After the one-year anniversary of Loren's death, I decide I'm ready to make an appointment with Tim, the medium. I vacillate between believing I'm crazy and thinking I'm adventurous. I imagine that's how the first astronauts felt when they boarded the space shuttle, not knowing where that quest would lead. One thing I know, though, is that Loren would applaud my courage since he was always eager for new adventures.

He was constantly admonishing me to seize every opportunity in life's fleeting moments whenever I was afraid to try something new, such as going to a channeler in Vancouver. On that occasion, a colleague of Loren's had recommended the channeler, who apparently had taken on the spirit of Spotted Eagle, a late-nineteenth-century Indian leader. Loren was interested immediately, and I, frightened, allowed myself to be persuaded to meet with the man, who, though at first looked and acted unremarkable went into a self-imposed trance then spoke in an entirely different manner. My dad had just died, and I asked the channeler where he was and if he was safe. His answer, spoken in words I did not understand, nevertheless calmed me. His most fitting response was when, in reply to Loren's question about his professional standing, Spotted Eagle told him to "stop caterwauling at the top of the mountain." Indeed, when Loren was feeling most ostracized he would do just that—except it was not on a mountain but to me. By the time the hour-long visit ended, I felt surprisingly soothed—like I had either been on a good drug trip or taken some Valium.

Loren himself took advantage of every challenge life had to offer, whether related to work, travel, or psychedelic experiences. Going to a medium feels more like it fits into the latter category. *Yet I did see Loren rising in the chapel. How did that happen?*

While deep in these memories, I dial the medium's number.

"Hi, this is Erin," says a cheerful voice.

"I would like to make an appointment with Tim," I answer before my good sense takes hold. "I've never done anything like this before, and I'm sorta scared."

"Oh, don't worry," Erin reassures me. "Tim is kind and warm."

*Sounds like a nanny or a puppy, not a medium.*

"Your job," she continues, "is to call forth the people you want to appear at the session. Tim will not ask who they are."

I make the appointment, hang up the phone, and feel very on edge, like I've had too much caffeine. *What if Loren comes? What if he doesn't come? What will it mean?* I still have no coherent belief about life after death, and I am hoping the experience will help me.

I decide I want my dad and Loren to come to the session, the two most important men in my life, who made me feel safe and loved. I sit on my bed with a picture of Loren in one hand and a picture of my dad in the other hand and say, "Okay, guys, I want you both there. But Dad, don't be offended, I want to spend more time with Loren." *Perhaps I will finally resolve the age-old Oedipal conflict.* I give them the date, hoping they will both be free, simultaneously realizing that anyone who is observing me would think I'm certifiably crazy. Unfortunately, the date of the appointment gets changed several times, and I go through my ritual, advising these two men of the change. The last time the date is changed I laugh and say, "Sorry, guys, but the date has been changed again. I know this is short notice. I hope you can fit this in your schedules and come to the session tomorrow."

I realize that just making the appointment implies I have decided, or at least hope, there is some sort of afterlife. *If only I could really know.*

The day of the session I feel nervous and fearful but excited—with butterflies in my stomach and perspiration drenching my armpits like a bride going to the altar. Today I want to look pretty; I dress for Loren in a long brown skirt, white peasant shirt, and camel-colored boots. Having lived in Verona, Italy, for a year, when I started wearing long skirts and boots Loren would joke that I was dressing like the beautiful women of Verona. "Judy," he would say with pride and delight, "you are my Veronese lady." I looked good in their sophisticated style and relished his obvious pleasure.

The meeting takes place in Encinitas, the same city where I meet my therapist and bereavement group—a good omen, I think.

"You won't have any trouble finding the place," Erin had told me. "It's a big two-story stucco house that Charlie Chaplin built for his mother." But I'm so anxious I drive past the address that I have clutched in my free hand.

I drive around the block again and finally find it. All I see is a big lawn curving around the front of a typical house. There is nothing that identifies it as a place that spirits from the afterlife might visit. My legs turn to jelly, and I have to force myself out of the car and onto the small porch, where there are a couple of broken-down beach chairs and a railing that, once white, is now chipped and mottled. The view from the porch is spectacular, with waves of the Pacific Ocean splashing onto the slightly graying beach sand.

I knock on the door. A younger woman greets me. "Hi, I'm Erin," she says as she grabs my hand in a firm handshake, "and you must be Judy."

"Yes," I say as I peg Erin as a new age person. She has very long black hair, wears brown Birkenstock sandals, a long, green broomstick skirt, and a white tank top with no bra. I feel very old as she leads me into the kitchen, which is surprisingly ordinary with a white porcelain four-burner stove and refrigerator, chipped white cabinets, and dishes drying in a white Rubbermaid dish rack. The pure whiteness of the kitchen adds a surreal quality to the experience.

Tim comes to greet me, his hand outstretched. Like the poster boy for college students who shop at the GAP, he is wearing khaki pants, a pale blue oxford button-down shirt, and Docksider boat shoes. *Is it possible this average-looking youngster who could be my son has extraordinary powers and is going to provide a new view of death?*

He leads me into another very ordinary-looking room with a three-cushion, tattered, light brown leather couch, a brown leather chair, a coffee table, tan scatter rugs, and several cats roaming around. The scent of sandalwood rises from a candle on the table.

I sit on the couch and am reminded of the first time I visited an analyst forty years before, when I experienced the same fear of the unknown. Yet with analysis I was trying to understand my own inner feelings and motivations. Here the quest looms larger—an understanding of the spirit world.

Tim says, "Judy, no words will pass between me and the spirits, but I will verbally communicate to you what they are saying." My anxiety and excitement are heightened. *Maybe I should have taken a Valium before coming here.*

"Although I may not understand what's being said, I will repeat it to you," he continues. "If you don't understand, however, ask me to get clarification." At that moment I want to leave, yet I'm rooted to the couch.

"Oh," he says, as if preparing to convey an afterthought, "the people who appear over your right shoulder will be your father's side of the family, those over your left shoulder will be your mother's side of the family, and those who appear behind you will be either your husband or friends."

I am hyperalert to everything he says but determined not to say anything that will give him clues.

"Someone is appearing over your right shoulder," he states, "someone who had heart problems. Does that mean anything to you?" My father had heart problems and died of a heart attack over eighteen years ago. My tears stun me. I forget that even though I am accustomed to my dad's absence I still miss him.

"He is thanking you for helping him along the way," Tim says. I understand. After my father died I learned that, according to the Jewish religion, each time the mourner's prayer is recited, the person who died is helped to a higher plane. So I went to temple every day for a month and then once a week for a year, each time reciting the mourner's prayer.

Tim continues, "Your father is holding his heart in a gesture to let me know how much he loves you." I feel comfort, as though someone had wrapped a soft, warm blanket around me.

"There is someone appearing behind you holding his liver. Did someone have liver problems?" Tim asks.

I feel my eyes open wide. "Yes, my husband died of liver cancer," I answer.

"Did this person also have kidney problems?" Tim asks.

"Yes again," I say. "Loren had dialysis just two days before he died." My heart pounds in my ears.

"He wants you to know his color is better and he now has strength in his legs." I sit there in stunned silence. I don't even think, I just am. Loren was yellow when he died, but I still don't want to say too much for fear of giving Tim information he can use.

"He wants you to know that even though you think he has not seen the new baby he has," says Tim. I start to cry. My stepdaughter gave birth to a baby boy, Jack Loren, approximately nine months after Loren died. When I first held this red-headed angel, I cried because Loren would never see this child, and now perhaps Loren has. Do Loren and my father really exist in spirit form, I wonder silently, my hopes rising.

Tim offers, as if describing two people meeting for coffee, "When Loren was going up, Jack was coming down, and they met in something similar to Grand Central Station." I try to envision such a place with both Loren and Jack there.

Tim continues, "He's smiling about Hawaii."

Incredible! Loren and I bought that condominium in Hawaii just before his diagnosis, and now he is smiling about it. I feel chills hearing Tim mention Hawaii, which seems to be something about which only Loren would know, after all. Tim then describes Loren laughing and spilling wine on my head. "Does that make sense to you?" he asks. The only thought that occurs to me is that Loren liked his wine and we always enjoyed a bottle of wine with our dinner. *Oh well, one loose end is not bad.*

"Your father just entered again," Tim says, "and he and Loren are joking with each other. But then your father apologized for coming back since he knows you want to spend more time with Loren." Holy cow, I think, this is the real thing. How could Tim possibly know that's what I told my father when I asked them both to come to this meeting? And how could my father have known that unless he heard me? Slowly I begin to entertain the possibility that there is some form of life after death on earth.

"Loren wants you to tell his daughter that he was sorry he could not die with her in the room. Her pull for him to stay on this earth was too strong. He is very emphatic about asking you to tell her this," Tim says to me. I understand. My mind briefly wanders back to Germany and the hospital where Loren died. I picture Missy coming to get me and describing how agitated Loren was during the time she was in the room. I promise I will do this.

"He says that you can learn a lot from his daughter," Tim continues. I don't know what this means. Missy works in the power world of Hollywood, something I would not want to do. Perhaps he is alluding to the developing relationship between us since he died. *If I could see him for only a minute. Maybe if he could just touch me, I won't look.*

"Loren is throwing his ring in your lap," Tim's voice continues, startling me out of the reverie.

I don't understand this. *Where did this ring come from? Is there a jewelry shop wherever he is? Or is this a generic sentence that Tim throws out to obtain an informational response?*

"Loren is pointing to a lovely lake that is near where he stands," Tim says. "They can take anything from their life on earth that is pleasing and make it part of their environment." *I wonder if I'm there. I hope so.*

"That makes perfect sense. One of Loren's happiest times of his youth was spent at Bass Lake, where his Uncle Ross taught him how to ride horses and how to pilot an airplane," I remark as I remember the Bass Lake T-shirt that's in the special drawer.

"I just asked Loren how you two met," Tim says in a voice tinged with laughter, "and he said it's none of my business." This brings a smile to my face as I remember our first night together, and our passionate lovemaking on the floor. I appreciate Loren's discretion.

Tim tells me that both Loren and my father say they had stayed on the earth longer than they were supposed to, for which I am thankful. Then just before the session ends, Tim tells me that Loren had his hands on my shoulders the whole time, a gesture of continuous love. I treasure the image.

After the session ends, I decide that it did not really help me understand the purpose of death but did make me feel calmer. My last images of Loren had been when he was bedridden and sick, when he died, and finally when he was rising off the bier, his destination not apparent. Now I can visualize him in the safe, beautiful place by the lake or running around with my father or other friends. Because of such images I feel freer.

Yet I am also left with many questions. Although my father was buried and Loren was cremated, they were both present. Although I didn't really sense their presence, when Tim translated their messages his information seemed accurate and I believed him. And when Tim described Loren with his hands on my shoulders, I did feel loved. My cynical friends might say that Tim could have googled me, but I don't have the same last name as Loren. And even if he did google me, he would not have known about Jack, Hawaii, that Loren did often stand behind me with his hands on my shoulders, or that I told my father I wanted to spend more time with Loren during the session. I still don't understand Loren's throwing his ring on my lap, but everything else was rooted in my reality.

Although I try to make sense of the experience, the spirit world remains a mystery. I wonder why Tim can access it and I cannot. Perhaps the reason why access to the spirit world is restricted is for self-protection. As much as I want to see Loren, maybe I could not function in this earthly world if I could call him forth whenever I wanted. And if Loren can really see what happens, if I do date and fall in love with another man will he be watching us make love together? Hopefully by then he will be settled in his own routine and too busy, or perhaps he will be cheering me on from the sidelines since I know he wants me to be happy.

# 8

# Going Ring Cold Turkey

*In the Symbol proper . . . there is ever, more or less distinctly and directly,
some embodiment and revelation of the Infinite;
the Infinite is made to blend itself with the Finite,
to stand visible, and as it were, attainable there.
By Symbols, accordingly, is man guided and commanded,
made happy, made wretched.*

*— Thomas Carlyle*

THE WORDS "WITH THIS RING I THEE WED," WHEN SPOKEN DURING A WEDDING ceremony, join together the lives of the bride and groom. The wedding ring is the archetypal image of infinite love and symbolic of the future hopes and dreams of the couple.

Most couples at the wedding ceremony do not, however, take to heart the potential implications of the last words of the ceremony: "Till death do us part." If every bride and groom really heard those words, weddings would be more somber, but who wants to think of death at the start of the party? I didn't.

But now I have to.

"Would you like a wedding band?" I asked Loren when we finally made the decision to get married.

"No," he said, his tone tinged with an anger I didn't understand, "I'm not going to feel like a person with a noose around his neck."

I was hurt. The purpose of getting married was to proclaim our mutual love, and, for me, the wedding ring symbolized that. "Okay, your decision, but I don't understand it. I know you had a nice gold wedding band the first time you were married because we cut it in half and had it made into earrings for Missy."

"Judy, the answer is no." I still didn't recognize the tone in his voice, but I knew to back off. It seemed that one of us was having wedding jitters, but I wasn't sure which one or why, since we had lived together for five years before making this decision. In fact, at the five-year mark we had had a caviar and champagne party to celebrate, as the invitation said, "five years of un-wedded bliss."

A month after our slightly contentious ring discussion we were in Big Sur, California. We stopped at Nepenthe, a restaurant with rustic tables over-looking the Big Sur coastline, with its white foam waves crashing against craggy rocks and turquoise ocean peeking through. Big Sur was a romantic spot for us since soon after meeting we had spent a week together there vis-iting friends, hiking, and making love. Nepenthe was also connected with good memories, as we had hosted Hal's rehearsal dinner there. After finish-ing our specialty Ambrosia burgers, a signature dish, and a couple glasses of New Zealand sauvignon blanc, we pulled ourselves away from the view and walked down the many steps toward our car.

"I'd like to stop in the gift shop before we leave," I said, lingering in front of the Phoenix Shop window.

"Okay," Loren said as we entered, "but hurry up. I want to get down off the mountain before the fog sets in."

"Fine," I replied, "I'll just do a quick look-through. You know I love to shop, and I just can't pass this up since we are here."

"I'll wait up by the jewelry counter," he answered.

The shop was filled with unique clothing and jewelry made by local arti-sans and artists from around the world. I walked by the soaps, picked up my favorite black Majorcan soap, Maja, and, as always, delighted in the sweet tangy smell of jasmine and rose. I perused the plaques with astrological signs and advice and read my horoscope, hoping to get some hint about our upcoming marriage. The predictions were all positive. I went down the stairs to the women's clothing area and checked out the T-shirts. Seeing nothing I wanted, I went back upstairs, worried that I'd taken too long and certain that Loren was already in the car. Instead, I was surprised to see him cradling a ring in his hand. I thought, maybe he was just pretending to hurry but wanted some time to look at rings for me.

"Isn't this exquisite?" he asked. I gulped when I realized it was a man's ring. The unique ring was square and flat across the top with a lapis lazuli stone embedded in gold and a thimbleful of amethyst shooting through the lapis lazuli at an angle.

"It's gorgeous," I said. Before I could stop myself, I asked, "Would you like me to buy it for you as a wedding ring?"

"Yes," he replied, and I don't know which of us was more surprised.

I waited until we were safely down the mountain before asking, with a peculiar tonal combination of child and adult, "When do I get to pick out my wedding ring?"

"You don't," he replied, mysteriously.

"What do you mean I don't? I only get married twice once," I responded, hoping to inject some humor into this conversation that had become too serious, "and I, too, would like to have a special ring for the occasion." How did we get here? I wondered. Loren didn't want a ring and now he has one, and I wanted one and didn't have one.

"I want to pick out your wedding band, and I want it to be a surprise for you. Can you live with that?" he asked as he took my hand in his free hand.

I looked at our hands joined together. *You want to pick out a ring for me? Haven't you noticed that I am an emancipated woman? I work, pay my share of the bills, make my own decisions, and I know what I like and dislike.* I closed my eyes so I could think. I trusted and loved this man. The romantic in me acknowledged that having him pick out my wedding band was exciting. Perhaps I didn't have to be emancipated every second. "Okay," I said, realizing that my life with Loren would be full of surprises.

When the day of our wedding arrived, I didn't give much thought to the ring. I was too busy directing caterers, hugging friends, and getting a last-minute massage from Danny, our good friend from Big Sur. Danny, with his black Coke bottle glasses, crooked smile, and long dark hair, was one of the photographers. He took a picture of the exact moment Loren placed the ring on my finger. It shows Loren with a smile on his face, his eyes crinkled with merriment, while my eyes are wide with surprise and happiness as I look at the ring, which featured a ruby set flat into 18-carat gold, with three tiny diamonds on each side. "This ring is so beautiful and yet so subtle," I said to Loren after the ceremony.

"I helped design it," Loren said as he smiled into my eyes. This ring, with its sparkling jewels, surely symbolizes the beginning of a wonderful married life for us, I thought to myself. And it did. Our marriage was unique and radiant, with a minimum of flaws, and lasted sixteen years until the cancer struck.

Right after Loren dies it never occurs to me not to wear the ring, but ten months later it's not so clear. Since there is still no book of rules I can follow, I call Sue.

"I've been having some very confusing thoughts, and I would like to run them by you," I say. "If I'm a widow, am I still married? Or does widowhood preclude the state of marriage? And if I'm not married why am I wearing my wedding ring? If I'm no longer married, I should not wear the ring on my left finger. Or is it that if I don't wear the ring on my left finger I'm no longer married?" I glance at the beautiful ruby-and-diamond ring, its sparkle a gentle reminder of past joys and yet somehow also a reproach about the future. For a second I imagine the ring asking me why I'm still wearing it. That thought seems no more absurd than the conversation we are having.

"Judy, you're driving yourself crazy. Remember what Loren used to say when there was a problem? 'Tincture of time.' Whether it was something about your mother or a simple rash on your skin, you always wanted to rush to a solution just to quell your anxiety, and Loren would always say, 'Judy, give the problem some time to heal itself. Use tincture of time.'"

"Okay, I'll sit with it since I can't think of any good solution right now," I respond before hanging up. Sue's advice brings back good memories of Loren's reassurance about the eventual healing of emotional wounds through time. I take the ring off for a second to test how it feels and look at the inside to see the inscription of our wedding date, wondering if I should add the date of his death, the end of the marriage on this earth. *But is the marriage over just because he died?* I am back where I started, missing Loren while looking at this symbol of our past happiness. I decide to wait until the year of mourning is up before making up my mind about the ring.

"I notice that you wear your wedding band on your thumb," I comment to Karenlee during one of our monthly dinners to share each other's journey through the grief process. Because she's a year ahead of me I'm always curious.

"It feels right for now. Did you know," she continued, "that in the olden days during the first year of mourning the widow wore black, during the second year gray, and during the third year lavender? Everything was clear and had rules. But in our advanced society we have no such rules, and so we have to make them up as we go along."

"Hard to know if we have moved forward or backward in our cultural perceptions and customs about death," I comment. I tell her of my struggle about the ring and my decision to wait.

After the first year following Loren's death, I take the wedding ring off my ring finger, where I have worn it for seventeen years, and put it in my red velvet jewelry box. That first morning without the ring I feel naked and vulnerable, sad and guilty, as though I have done something wrong. Just when I think my feeling plate is overflowing, another feeling appears — betrayal. Am I betraying our love? I wonder. *Yet Loren did throw his ring in my lap at that session with the medium. Perhaps that makes sense after all. Was he giving me permission to take off my wedding ring and move on?*

The phrase "With this ring I thee wed" goes through my mind, reminding me of our devotion to each other, our earthly connection. But then I remember the phrase "Till death do us part," which implies that a marriage ends when one of the partners dies. That doesn't help much. I feel like I'm in my boat in the middle of an ocean with all anchors up and without my GPS. I don't know where I'm going. With the change from wife to widow, I have gone from crew member to captain, from luxury liner to dinghy, yet I still feel confident that I will be able to navigate the rough waters ahead. And I still have my metaphorical life raft, my good instincts and my ability to plan.

I make no more decisions about the ring for several months. Reflecting my ambivalence, some mornings I put it on my ring finger, and it feels like home, but then I remember that home, as I knew it, no longer exists, take the ring off, and feel a deep loneliness.

One day Sue calls and asks, "So, what're you doing about the ring?"

"Okay, you are for sure gonna think I'm crazy." I no longer wear the ring, but I feel like I need to recondition, or regroove, my fingers. I think my fingers need to realize that the situation is changing and there are no more predictable ring rituals."

"First Loren's clothes have feelings; now your fingers need regrooving," she says, laughing. "Are you sleeping okay? Are you on drugs?"

"Yes, I'm sleeping fine, and no I'm not taking drugs," I answer, laughing too, as her laughter is contagious. I never thought I would be able to laugh about anything that had to with Loren's death. I continue, "Here's my plan. I'm going ring cold turkey. I won't wear any rings for several months. That way my fingers will know there is going to be a big change."

"Whatever works," she concludes.

I keep my fingers in training for their new ring life from July until Christmas. I feel naked without the ring, but I get used to it. At Christmas I go to a jeweler and have the ring sized for the fourth finger of my right hand.

"Whoa," I tell Karenlee at one of our monthly dinners, "I sure underestimated the emotional impact of getting this ring resized."

"What do you mean?" she asks, still wearing her wedding band on her thumb.

"Somehow I thought since I'm aware of what I'm doing it's no big deal. I didn't realize the power of the ring. Now I not only feel like I'm in the middle of the ocean alone but that someone took my life raft. I really have to find my sea legs, or sea fingers. I'm not really afraid of drowning. It's just a matter of treading water or learning new strokes to get back to my life raft until I feel more comfortable with this new identity."

I begin to wear the ring on my right fourth finger. It feels awkward and wrong, but I persist. *Should I wear it every day? If I don't, am I being disloyal? But how can I be disloyal to someone who is dead?* After this experiment, I understand that the symbolism of the ring is so powerful that changing hands does not break the connection. The connection between husband and wife is so strong that the bond continues, although in a different manner, after the death of one of them. It becomes obvious to me that, with or without the ring, Loren will always be an important part of both my past and current life. Although there are concrete things I learned from him that influence my life today, like love of opera and travel, it is the more subtle continuation of his love that still endures and supports me, an unseen cushion I can fall onto when necessary.

One day I ask Sue, "I sort of resolved my ring problem, now what do I do about Loren's wedding ring?"

"Judy, what are you thinking?"

"Well, I tried it on my left index finger, and it looks and feels good. It's that beautiful lapis lazuli color, and I just bought a small blue heart that same color. I wear them together and feel like I'm mixing 'something old, something new,' like I'm integrating the parts of my old life with my new life. I realize that I can't and don't want to erase Loren from my life in order to move on. That would leave such hollowness in my heart."

"Sounds like a solution," she says, "but what about all the other rings Loren had?"

"Oh, Suz, I'm not sure I'm ready to face those." I hang up the phone and open up Loren's tan leather jewelry box. Loren loved his jewelry as he loved his clothes, and each of the many rings is associated with a memory. I pick up the yellowish green peridot ring that I purchased from the women's jewelry department in Tiffany's. I look at the emerald ring that I gave him on one of our anniversaries, and the onyx ring I had custom made for his seventieth birthday, with the simple inscription "pal" and the date. I close my eyes and let the unsummoned memories surface.

When Loren was sixty-five, my mother gave him an onyx ring that he liked. The Christmas before his seventieth birthday he lost the ring in the pillows of one of our children's couches. When we searched and couldn't find it, we figured the dog swallowed it. There was no way to get it that we were willing to pursue.

I knew he missed this black ring. It was the one he wore the most and the one that drew a lot of attention, so I decided to have one made for his seventieth birthday as a surprise.

The summer before his September birthday, we were in Santa Fe. I shopped for a dress for the big birthday party in a shop similar to the one in Nepenthe where I had bought Loren's wedding band. The dress fit like a glove, was a showcase for my good figure, and the soft material caressed me. It was the first time in weeks that I had felt so good because at the time I was depressed about my mother, who had just developed breast cancer and was in a downward spiral with dementia. In addition, I was worried about Loren turning seventy since my dad had had his first heart attack on his seventieth birthday.

"Whatdya think?" I asked, twirling around to give Loren a view from every angle while he waited at the jewelry counter.

"You look gorgeous, and remember that the single most helpful thing for depression is shopping," my psychiatrist husband replied with a twinkle. Then he said, "Look at this black onyx ring and tell me what you think."

I hesitantly turned the ring over in my hand so it looked like I was carefully inspecting it, but I was actually buying time to think of an answer so he wouldn't purchase a ring similar to the one I had planned to give him as a birthday gift.

"It's beautiful. But don't you think you have enough rings, and besides this one is not that great," I finally answered, keeping my fingers crossed as I lied my way through this maze. I breathed a sigh of relief as Loren seemed to lose interest in the ring, and we walked out of the store.

"I can't believe I was so naive as to think Loren, who is incredibly attentive and intuitive, would let it go," I told Sue as I was recounting the story after our return home.

"So what happened?" she asked.

"Well, we were walking through the streets and holding hands, when Loren turned to me, smiled, and said in the hushed tone of a secret between lovers, "I know you're getting me a new black ring for my birthday."

"Why on earth would he think that?" Sue wondered.

"Those were my exact words to him, except I added a denial. But he called my bluff, saying, 'Okay, then, I'll go back and buy that black ring.' We both started to laugh," I recounted, giggling again at the memory.

I open my eyes and am shocked to find myself alone in the room, as the memory of Loren had been so vivid. I wipe away the tears and gaze at this ring. How can I get rid of a ring that in its tiny circumference holds so much history? I realize I'm not ready to do that. I put the rings back in the jewelry box where their history is safe and decide they will stay there until I'm ready to size them for myself or give them away.

The following Christmas I'm standing with my six-foot-tall son-in-law, David Lee, who's dressed in red basketball shorts and a gray T-shirt. The presents have been opened, and there is a moment of quiet.

"Judy," he says, "even though I don't talk much about Loren I think about him every day. I tell my friends what an important influence he was in my life." I look up at his serious face and see the sadness in his eyes.

"I know," I say in a soft voice and give him a big hug. Suddenly, I want David Lee to have a piece of his father-in-law, something to treasure just as he treasured Loren.

I go home and decide to give David Lee one of Loren's rings for his thirty-ninth birthday. I take the rings out again and look at them. I cannot let go of the wedding ring or of the black onyx ring I had made for his seventieth birthday yet. But I send to David Lee another black ring with tiny diamonds in the shape of an L that I had made for Loren's sixtieth birthday.

At my sixty-fifth birthday party, two weeks after David Lee's birthday, he pulls me aside, looking handsome in his bright blue shirt, black jacket, and pressed jeans. "I just wanted you to see this," he says, as he holds his right hand out and displays the ring on his pinky finger.

"I'm glad," I respond as tears start to form in my eyes, "I hoped it would be right."

David Lee goes back to join the merriment. I linger for a moment, realizing that something important has occurred—I gave away a piece of Loren and don't feel empty. I gave away the ring but not the memories of his sixtieth birthday party. Like Loren's clothing, his wedding band and other jewelry are symbols, which although helpful for triggering memories, do not contain the memories themselves.

I am the container for those.

# 9

# Blindsided by Valentine's Day

*To Loren —*
*Long ago . . . in the Land of Oz*
*I saw you*
*Leaning against a wall*
*Silent*
*But there.*
*Soon after, I was summoned.*
*I appeared on your doorstep*
*At 2 a.m.*
*Carrying a daisy . . .*
*"He likes me, he likes me not."*
*Who could have predicted that so many years later*
*We would be sharing so much —*
*Love, laughter, sex, sadness,*
*Life!*
*You are my friend, my lover,*
*My . . . voluptuary!*
*Today I bring you daisies*
*In honor of those young lovers*
*From so many years ago . . .*
*Who are still together.*

*With love, Judy*

*2/14/2004*


"I guess I thought Valentine's Day would not be a problem, so I wasn't prepared," I tell Bev. She wears a caramel-colored sweater that accentuates her kind brown eyes. The sun shines through the window, illuminating the highlights in her fawn-colored hair.

"What happened?" she asks.

"Valentine's Day was really difficult. I sent the kids Valentine cards and gifts last week and didn't give it a second thought. I figured that by now, more than halfway through the second year after Loren died, I wouldn't have a problem. I realized how naive I was when I had to force myself out of bed yesterday. It reminded me of the day after my divorce, when I refused many invitations for Christmas dinner, figuring that since I was Jewish that day would not be a big deal. Then on Christmas day I felt so alone that I eventually did go to a friend's house. But Valentine's Day is the one day in the whole year when couples and love are celebrated, with few options for people without a relationship. Sadness and loneliness washed over me all day like a neverending tsunami. I thought of Loren all day. I cried as I reread the poem I wrote for him for the last Valentine's Day we shared, then replayed in my mind the whole four months of his illness and death."

"How did you spend the evening?" Bev inquires.

"The movie club I belong to had a 'Special Valentine's Day Treat'—an IMAX movie about Greece and Greek culture." I visualized myself a single-ton amongst the couples—a leafless tree in a green forest. *Did anybody notice me? Did anybody really care?*

"So, how was it to go to the movies alone on Valentine's Day?"

"Awful. I have no problem going to the movies alone. But on Valentine's Day? I didn't go to celebrate but just to keep busy until the twenty-four hours passed. The couples laughed, held hands, and acted as if they had a secret. I was one of the few single people there and felt very alone. I wanted to yell out that one of them might die before the next Valentine's Day and they should cherish each moment they are together."

"How do you feel today, Judy?" Bev asks gently.

"I feel defeated, as if I've been studying for an exam for a long time and then fail it. I thought that after almost two years I was past the major part of my grief since I haven't been thinking of Loren every minute of every day, but apparently I'm not as healed as I had hoped. The poultice of traveling, taking courses, and visiting friends has been successful at helping me live a new life, but underneath there is still a wound, perhaps one that will never fully heal."

"Judy, you were blindsided by Valentine's Day," Bev answers sympathetically. "You prepare well for the anniversaries and days you think will be difficult, but since you thought this Valentine's Day was not a big deal you ignored it. Do you remember how you and Loren spent your last Valentine's Day? Perhaps that will give us a clue as to what made yesterday so troublesome."

"I hardly remember a thing about last year except that I got through it," I reply, grabbing a tissue to blot my tears. "But the last Valentine's Day Loren and I spent together I remember well. It was on that day that Loren went to the hospital to have the first test to discern the site of bleeding. I sat there so nervous, the minutes dragging on and on, until Dr. Sunder came out in his green surgical scrubs with his face mask pulled down. He said the procedure had gone well, that he had seen some swellings on the esophagus. I was so relieved because that could account for the bleeding, but then he went on to say he saw something 'funny' and he scheduled a biopsy. Then I got really scared as I always associate the word *biopsy* with cancer."

"Did you and Loren talk about that later?"

"No. When I went up to the recovery room, he was trying to button his shirt but couldn't line up the buttons with the holes. I made some joke about butterfingers, and he just glared at me. We didn't talk at all on the way home, and when we got home he quickly went to sleep, I now think because he was apprehensive about the results."

It's uncomfortable to relive these memories, but I know Bev's idea is on target: if I can understand what was difficult about that last Valentine's Day, perhaps I will understand some of my feelings about this past one. And maybe I will also learn something more about the grieving process, especially why unanticipated feelings sometimes erupt unexpectedly like a volcano.

"What about your Valentine's Day poem?" Bev asks, probingly.

I hesitate before answering, as the pain is raw, like a new burn. Then I say, "I heard him get up and was excited to present my poem to him, along with the daisies I had bought to commemorate our first time together. But he went into his office and started to shuffle papers and work on taxes. I was furious and yelled, 'I can give up Valentine's Day for the medical tests but not for the damn taxes.'"

My tears interrupt my voice. I catch my breath then continue, "Loren did come out after I yelled at him, looking shrunken and old. I read the poem to him, and we both cried. I think we both had forebodings about the future but couldn't share them at that point. I kept waiting for him to bring out a card, flowers, or some gift. I, like most romantics, always looked forward to Valentine's Day, and he had always presented me with a gift and a card revealing a handwritten sentiment at the bottom. But this day I received nothing. I felt ignored and angry at a time when I needed to feel loved and, most importantly, safe. Finally, he said in a low voice, 'Babe, I'm so sorry. I didn't get you anything for Valentine's Day. I guess that's what happens when you leave things for the last minute.' He tried a weak smile. I smiled back, but I was so enraged my hands shook. I kept thinking what's the big deal to go out and buy a card or flowers? I felt like I was an adolescent who did all the right things to be popular but nobody seemed to notice. I allowed myself several minutes of self-pity and then realized that Loren, as a physician, was more aware of the meaning of the test results than I was . . . and he didn't want to talk about it. It was more painful for me to be shut out than not to receive a card or flowers."

"Sounds like you were very hurt but didn't want to express it," Bev observes.

"Yeah, I knew Loren was suffering, too, but I had learned not to push him to talk. We did salvage some of the evening. We sat down to eat the special dinner I had prepared—scallops marinated and cooked in ginger, soy sauce, and cilantro—and after guessing that it was a Martha Stewart recipe, Loren remarked playfully, 'You know, Judy, Martha Stewart has done more for the ginger, cilantro, and soy sauce industry than anyone else.' This was a joke between us, and we both laughed. Loren knew that every month I carefully read each recipe in Martha Stewart's magazine and cut out the relatively easy ones so when it was my time to do the cooking I had a stash from which to choose. He was particularly tickled with my slavish devotion to the exact directions and proportions in the recipes and Martha Stewart's consistent use of those particular flavorings. Our laughter cut through the tension, and I was relieved for that moment. I wonder if I had known that was to be our last Valentine's Day whether I would have done anything differently. I think not, but I also think that sometimes it's a curse to look back."

Bev remarks, "Maybe the reason Valentine's Day is so difficult this year is not only that it's a day for couples and love but because for you it was the beginning of the end. Judy, I can see by your face that despite your acceptance you still feel Loren's death is unfathomable."

"Yes, I do. I'm having fun, and in some ways I'm the 'merry widow' Loren predicted. But it is still unfathomable that Loren is not here, and despite my visit to Tim, the medium, I don't really know where he is."

"Yes, as one of my patients said when I worked in hospice, death is a thief."

"Sure is. Death takes away everything, leaving only memories. There's no chance of catching this thief and no court of law to file claims for damages."

After I leave Bev's office, I continue to reflect on our session. I realize that I still can't believe I will never see Loren again. And Valentine's Day just underscored his absence even more. There are so many things I want to tell him, places I've visited, experiences I've had, and insights about our life together. It seems silly to think I have learned something new about our relationship after he died, but I have. Some lines from the play *I Never Sang for My Father*, which I saw when I was twenty-five, come to mind: "Death ends a life, but it does not end a relationship, which struggles on in the survivor's mind toward some resolution which it may never find."

I don't know what resolution I'm looking for, because the only real resolution would be for Loren to come back, and that is never going to happen.

When I get home, I sit down in my writing room, look at the small bottle of ashes on the shelf, and write a letter to Loren:

*Dear Pal,*

*It's the day after Valentine's Day, and I'm still having a rough time. I keep thinking of things I want to tell you. I want you to know that several of your colleagues came to the house last month to look at your research data and consider doing a follow-up study of the Soteria residents. And that weekend I learned more about our relationship, or at least realized how lucky I was to have you in my life. Tom, always serious, was the designated chef, and Debra, his life partner, as you know, and I had the task of shopping. "What do you want to make for dinner?" she asked him before we left.*

*"Some kind of fish, not salmon," he answered as he kissed her good-bye. We approached the fresh fish vendor in the same open-air market where we used to go every Saturday morning. "I love salmon," I told Debra. "Why don't we buy this?" "I wish we could," she said with downcast eyes, "but Tom said not to get salmon." So we bought halibut and scallops and returned home. I overheard Debra say to Tom, "They had the most beautiful salmon there."*

*"Why didn't you buy it?" he asked. At that instant, I realized that one of the treasures of our relationship was that you were the least controlling person I knew. You were always clear in your communications, and you never tried to control any situation or me. I know you had your preferences, but we were able to negotiate everything, even on that last Valentine's Day when I yelled at you. I hope you know, somewhere in that vast unknown called death, that I appreciate the fact that you loved me and trusted me enough not to try to control me.*

*That same weekend Paul was scheduled to take a late plane to snow-bound New York City. I was certain he wasn't going to make his plane.*

*"Call the airport and find out if your plane is leaving," I kept bugging him all day. Sound familiar?*

*"There's nothing I can do about that. It will either go or it won't," he responded—the very words I heard from you when I used to bug you about something over which you had no control. In that moment, I really appreciated the fact that you tolerated a lot of my attempts at control, without getting angry. You just quietly pointed out to me that I could not control the world.*

I put the pen down and close my eyes for a minute to organize my thoughts. What else do I want to tell him? I pick up the pen and continue:

*I now sleep on my side of the bed only. I know you may find that hard to believe since in addition to calling me a "space-occupying lesion" you used to call me a "bed hog." I miss our laughter in bed when you would pull my hand over your naked body and place it on the edge of the bed saying, "See how much room you left me?" I just wanted to be close to you. When I would neverthe-*

*less roll over on my side of the bed, and you would nudge me even further to
the edge, then it would be my turn to take your hand over my nude body and
show you how close to the edge of the bed I was. You might find it funny that
now I stay on my side of the bed and don't spread out at all. The reason I stay
on my side of the bed, however, is not funny. It's too painful to experience the
emptiness of the other side of the bed, and the emptiness inside me that is most
apparent at night.*

I debate whether I want Loren to know I finally wrote to his gastroenter-
ologist complaining about how he treated Loren when providing the original
diagnosis. He would probably think that was controlling and say something
like, "Judy, just let it be." But I didn't always follow his advice, and he accepted my decisions even if he didn't agree with them. I continue:

*I never told you how furious I was with Dr. Sunder after he gave you your
diagnosis over the telephone, as if it were a confirmation of some mail-order
invoice, and then refused to give you an appointment to discuss the biopsy and
told you there was nothing he could do. But writing a letter to him helped me
let it go. And the bonus was that he called me and apologized for his thought-
lessness and said he had learned the importance of communicating better with
his patients.*

Should I tell him I'm thinking about travel? Would he be jealous? I can
only guess at his reactions, and jealousy would not likely be one. I go on:

*Loren, every day of this seemingly endless journey through grief I struggle
to identify what role you will play in my future life. How do I continue with
my life—let go of you and yet hold on to you at the same time? The struggle
now is how to say so long but not good-bye. I feel like a dancer doing the
splits, with my body stretched in half yet connected. I think you will be happy
to know I am not falling over. But you wouldn't be surprised; you always
commented on my strength. How I wish we could be sitting up late at night,
drinking wine and talking about these things. But then, if we could do that I
wouldn't be having these feelings. Every day I think of some aspect of our life
together, usually with smiles, often with sadness, sometimes with anger about
how you could have left me.*

How do I sign this letter that probably will never be received? I obsess for a few more minutes, reluctant to let go of what became an intense communication that made it feel like Loren was present, and decide no signature is necessary. I reread the letter and to my surprise have no tears on my face but feel lighter. The writing helped. Finally, I add a mischievous postscript to the letter:

> *P.S. I think I am going to write a book about becoming a widow. I wasn't going to tell you about it, but I feel so close to you now, as if you are here in the room with me. I know you would never laugh at my ideas, only support me . . . and that's one thing I continue to miss.*

I fold the letter, slide it into an envelope, and place it in the special drawer.

After tucking away my love letter, I take a photo of Loren off my dresser, a great picture of him with his bright blue eyes and smile staring at me. I feel like he is watching me every minute, and Valentine's Day made it that much more difficult to look at the photo. Paradoxically, I don't want to see him every moment yet I want to see him all the time. *Contradictions. More/less, life/death. Happiness/sadness.* I feel like I have one arm holding Loren tight, like a little girl clutching her first doll, and the other arm wide open, leaving me surprised and frightened when the doll falls.

I ask myself if we could spend just one more hour or one more day together what questions would I ask Loren: Do you love me? Do you miss me? Did you enjoy our time on this earth together? But I already know the answers to all these questions—yes, yes, and yes.

So what do I want? I don't want to feel the pain. Yet if I don't feel the pain I don't feel Loren. And if I feel too much pain I am paralyzed and don't move forward. If I move forward, am I leaving him behind? Do I have to leave him behind so that I can move forward? Sometimes I feel like an amateur juggler, but instead of balls or flames I juggle all these conflicting feelings of my life—up in the air, down again, trying to catch them, often dropping one, then having to take a deep breath and try again.

And all these feelings were evoked because I got blindsided on Valentine's Day—that day when Cupid and Eros are celebrated, couples walk hand in hand, men wear red ties with hearts on them while women wear red dresses, and couples who seem to adore each other fill the restaurants.

But for me it is still a day I again have to face the fact, with some disbelief, that I will never see Loren again.

# 10

# The Penis Test

*Women desire six things. They want their husbands to be
brave, wise, rich, generous, obedient to wife, and lively in bed.*

— *Geoffrey Chaucer*

"I'VE BEEN THINKING A LOT ABOUT WHAT IT WILL BE LIKE TO MEET ANOTHER MAN and even sleep with him," I tell Sue during one of our weekend conversations. I'm almost embarrassed to be thinking about such a thing, but I also want to try this new idea out with her.

"Are you keeping secrets from me?" comes the hurt voice of my friend. "Did you meet someone?"

"Of course not. Chet down the block has been creeping me out by telling me how good I look and giving me the cat whistle, but it made me think it might not be so bad to meet a nice guy. Anyway, I have this great idea! If you think regrooving my fingers is weird, wait'll you hear this one," I reply.

"I'm ready. Nothing shocks me," Sue says with anticipation.

"Let me grab the teakettle, and I'll tell you." I cradle the phone between my shoulder and my neck while pouring hot water from the teakettle into a cup containing my Tension Tamer tea bag.

"Well," I start tentatively, "I'm trying to figure out some private way to decide whether I want to see a guy again or, more importantly, have sex with him. So I have developed something I call the penis test." I know I'm making a joke about a serious problem, but humor makes it easier.

"Get out," Sue responds.

I continue, "It goes something like this: When I meet a man, I try to picture him naked and think about how his penis looks. If I visualize it as attractive, then it's a go; if not, then no. I think I sort of did that with Chet but not consciously. I think I did it with Ben as well. Of course, with Loren I just looked at his seductive eyes and was captured." For a second I envision Loren standing nude after a shower, with droplets of water all over, just before wrapping a towel around his waist and covering the good parts.

I pull myself back to the present as Sue asks, "Who's Ben?"

"Y'know, the member of the group that met daily at the coffee shop. The first time I met him was at Loren's sixty-fifth birthday party. He was elegantly dressed in a pin-striped suit, and with his British accent I thought he was attractive. I was particularly moved that he brought his wife, who was then suffering from dementia, to the party and was so gentle with her. He invited us to some musical salons at his house, and each time I saw him I was impressed with his charm and wit. When his wife died, Loren and I went to the ceremony. Then several months later Loren died, and I gave him a hug at Loren's memorial service, saying, "Who would have believed this?" referring to the proximity of his wife's and Loren's deaths. By that time I realized that he wore his pin-striped suit all the time and he didn't seem so special."

"Oh, now I remember you went out with him. Remind me what happened," Sue says.

I recall how anxious I was before that date, then continue, "He asked me to join him and some other couples from the coffee group for dinner. I figured I might as well start with someone I knew. It turned out to be pretty boring, with three couples, women on one side, men on the other. Loren and I never did that; when we went out with other couples, we always sat interspersed, not like school kids on a bench. By the end of the evening, I didn't find him very attractive, and I was so nervous that he was going to kiss me I jumped out of the car before it came to a total stop. Besides, his car was pretty dirty with lots of papers strewn about, dust everywhere, and stuff in the backseat."

"Hey," Sue says, "maybe you should have the car test in addition to the penis test."

"Are you making fun of me?" I reply.

"No, I just remember that when you told me about the evening you wondered why you were getting into that car—in fact, your exact words were 'Where is my chariot, and where is my Prince Charming?'"

"Well, that was six months ago. It was too soon, and I've grown up since then. Soon after that date he sent an e-mail asking if I would like to go up to Huntington Beach to spend some time at the museum. I had never been there and might have considered it if it had been a day trip, but it was an overnight trip. And even weirder was the fact that he proposed we stay in one room with two separate beds. Separate rooms might have worked for me. Of course, that was after he showed me the 'fornification room' in his house." I laugh to myself, acknowledging that at least each new experience, while terrifying at the time, has helped me develop this theory that I am now discussing with Sue.

"That was all pretty weird," Sue concedes, "showing you the room, wanting to go away, yet saying you could have separate beds. Glad you said no to that one. Yeah, I know he also failed the penis test."

"Now you're catching on," I answer, taking a sip of tea.

"Getting back to the Judy Schreiber Penis Test, have you thought about the fact that most of the men you meet will be older and not the hoped for Adonis of our youth?" Sue asks, ever practical.

"I have and I realize that another advantage of growing older with somebody is that the first flush of love and lust are saved in what I call the memory bank. I think we rarely look objectively at the body of our beloved. When I looked at Loren's seventy-year-old body, I know what I perceived was influenced by thirty years of love. Lots of times in these last few years when I picked him up at the airport, I was always surprised that the 'old, tired man' waving me down was actually Loren. Then we would start talking, and by the time we went to bed he was 'my Loren' and I couldn't wait to be held by him. Somehow my mind retained the image of the body of the person I had fallen in love with thirty years earlier. I don't know how that can happen with someone I just met."

As we are talking, I walk into the bathroom and look at the old picture of Loren and me nude in a dinghy, he holding a bucket over his penis and me demurely covering all my parts with my arms. I smile at the memory and tell

Sue, "I would like the next nude male body I see to be compact and firm — not an Adonis but not an Archie Bunker either. But then I look at myself in the mirror and realize I have sags and wrinkles where there used to be only clear, flat skin. There's no solution I can think of short of turning off the lights."

Suddenly I recall how, after the divorce from my first husband, I kept wondering if I would ever be really happy. Then when I met Loren, I knew he could help me find happiness, not the unreal perfection of so many Hollywood movies but a deeper sense of love and contentment. He was honest, nonjudgmental, caring, and knew how to have fun. Also, he passed my secret test to determine if a man was a true mate: if I woke up in the middle of the night, looked over at him crumpled up, snoring, or dribbling, and could still smile and feel jelly inside. I even felt that way with Loren in the hotel in Germany when he was dying.

"Judy, you will figure this out if and when you meet the right man," Sue replies, her voice full of encouragement.

"Maybe. Right now when I think of 'the right man' it is mostly a replica of Loren, and that's not going to happen. Maybe it has to be someone totally different so I don't constantly make comparisons. And the thought of going to bed with someone new is both titillating and terrifying."

"Judy, you have to start somewhere. You'll just have to wait and see. You can't control everything, as Loren used to say," Sue reminds me and we hang up. I finish my tea and place the empty cup in the sink.

Several months later my friend Stan asks me if he can give my phone number to a friend of his named Rob. *What do I do now? It's too soon. Really, it's almost two years? What if I hate him? What if I like him? Remember, Sue said you have to start somewhere.* I say yes. I know I need to meet other men and practice dating.

Rob calls, and we make a date to meet at a restaurant for dinner. *Good start — a restaurant Loren and I never went to but of the same caliber.* I feel calm, don't obsess about dress, makeup, or even the zit that appears on my face. I have a serious chat with myself and decide to not to be too quick to judge.

I get there early, but he is already there. He's about six feet tall, has gray hair, very fair skin, and an Irish accent. *Irish accent is a plus, reminds me of Loren when he used to say in an Irish brogue, "Me mother's name was O'Brien."* I notice that while not an elegant snappy dresser like Loren, Rob is dressed nicely but conservatively, in slacks of indeterminate color, a light blue tie, and dark blue blazer. His palm is damp when we shake hands, and I assume he is as nervous as I. *Loren's palm was never damp. I used to love it when we were driving somewhere and he would gently pick up my hand and hold it. I felt so loved. Stop the comparisons. It's only been two minutes, and already there are three of us on this date: me, Rob, and Loren.*

We have a nice dinner accompanied by the usual first-date often boring comparing of notes about our lives. *I feel like I'm in a sitcom. George Costanza from Seinfeld on a first date.* It goes well, but he fails the penis test—nice man but no chemistry. When he calls to ask me out again, however, I decide to give it a try.

"Good for you, Judy," Sue says when I tell her about the upcoming second date. "Maybe you'll find out you like him, and then he'll pass the penis test, after all."

"Don't know, but thanks for the encouraging words. I'll call you after the date."

We meet at a friendly neighborhood bar, to be followed by dinner at a restaurant down the block. We share stories, have a drink, share stories again, and leave for the restaurant no more than two minutes away.

"Then Mr. Failed the Penis Test took my hand," I report to Sue later, "so we can walk hand in hand to the restaurant, and I wanted to tell him that I am an anti-Beatle, that I don't wanna hold his hand. It was limp and damp—perhaps a test I can use in the future is the hand test. It's funny, because I used to love it when Loren and I would walk hand in hand. I don't think it was the holding hands that bothered me but the dampness and limpness." I start to giggle. "Sounds like I could be describing a penis. Okay, I'll get hold of myself, so to speak." I'm once again surprised that I can laugh about a situation that is so connected to Loren's death.

"So, didya pull your hand away?" Sue asks, anxiously awaiting the outcome.

"C'mon, Sue, I'm a well-brought-up girl. I thought it would be rude and infantile of me not to hold this man's hand until we got to the restaurant. I just repeated to myself, silently, 'Surely, Judy, you can do this without ruining your life.' "

"I'm proud of you," she replies supportively.

"I was so relieved when we reached the restaurant. I figured the worst had passed and now I could enjoy a good Italian meal. Then just when I started to relax he put his hand across the table to hold mine. 'Get your hands off me, bud. The only person who is allowed to touch me is Loren,' I thought to myself."

"Yeah, but he's dead," Sue adds.

I'm jolted for a second by Sue's forthrightness but then realize I had the same thought, although hearing it out loud seems different.

"My thought exactly. Nevertheless, I managed to keep my hands as busy as I could and, as I was taught when I was little, I kept them on my side of the table. Suddenly a line from Act IV of *Macbeth* seeped into my already anxious brain: 'All the perfumes of Arabia will not sweeten this little hand.'"

"Your mother would be proud, Judy, that your education did not go to waste."

"Stop, and listen to what happened. I know it's comical, but going out with someone else is a big deal. Besides, my sense of humor gets me through the tough times. Anyway, after the appetizers were removed, he reached across the table, took my hand, and said, 'I bet we could make beautiful love together.'"

"You're kidding. What did you say?" asks Sue.

"Not on your life, buster!" I laugh. " 'No,' I simply said, 'You know, I am not ready for that.' So now I have a guy who failed the penis test, the hand test, and the newly identified speaking test. The longest dinner finally ended, and we walked back to my car, where he asked me to give him a ride home."

"Uh-oh," Sue interrupts. "No car. He failed the car test as well."

"It's not that simple. I stopped in his driveway, left the car running, and waited for him to get out. Instead, he turned to me and said, 'Can I have a good night kiss?' My personal theory is if you have to ask for a kiss the answer is no, but I was curious."

"You actually kissed him?" Sue asks.

"He bent over, and I wondered if I should close my eyes or keep them open. I closed them and then peeked—his eyes were closed. The kiss felt weird, like wearing someone else's clothes. I knew it wouldn't be the same as Loren kissing me, but I didn't think it would feel that alien. Loren always puckered up and kissed with confidence; this was just a flat pair of lips on mine." The image of Loren puckering up that last morning before he died comes uninvited into my head. I sweep my free hand across my forehead to get rid of it.

"Well, you did it," Sue responds. "So you're over the hurdle of kissing a man."

"True, but then he asked for another kiss. For a second I was an adolescent again, but I realized that I'm an adult and can say no, which is what I did. He asked me to call him when I get back from New York."

"Are you going to do that?" Sue asks, but in a voice that intuits the answer.

"Nope," I reply. "Being an adult is pretty good. I have lots of choices and no adolescent shoulds."

"My, aren't we the philosopher," Sue teases before saying good-bye.

*I hate this. I don't want to date anyone else. But I don't want to spend the rest of my life without a man either. Or do I? Loren and I had such a magical relationship that it will be difficult to be with someone else.* I decide to stop thinking about all these possibilities. At the moment I am alone, without male prospects, so why worry. Loren was right. I can't control the world, although I sure would like to.

A couple of months after the first kiss experience I'm on a plane to Hawaii. I luxuriate in the extra room in business class and immediately take out a book, my shield against having to talk to anybody. When I hear a loud voice, I look up and see a guy about seventy years old with a rugged, sun-weathered face talking to everyone as he meanders down the aisle. He's wearing jeans, a beige crewneck, and sneakers, and has to duck under the open overhead bins to avoid bumping his head. He stops at my row, puts his black and red backpack in the overhead bin, and sits next to me. I keep my book up and head down, hoping he doesn't want to talk.

"I just returned from Switzerland," he says as he turns in his seat toward me. I smile politely. "Security was hell because of my hip replacement."

*Damn, he's a talker. Keeping my head in a book is not going to work.* I tell him my experience bringing back ashes from Germany. I want people to know I'm a widow, and yet it's a difficult thing to weave into a conversation.

"Did you say ashes?" he repeats, looking startled.

"Yes, my husband died in Germany a couple of years ago, and I had to bring his ashes through security."

"My wife died five months ago," he says.

To my surprise we talk during the entire six-hour flight—about death, traveling alone, eating alone, and mourning. I learn that he had been married for fifty years and his wife died of cancer. I learn that his daughter died eight years before. I learn that he had two hip replacements and survived one bout of prostate cancer. I learn that as I look at this man I cannot imagine being in bed with him. He passes the talk test but not the penis test.

Even so, I enjoy the journey. The stewardess looks at us with a smile that implies she senses the blossoming of a new romance. I keep looking at her looking at us and think, "Not on your life." I'm aware of little things that turn me off, like the fact that he keeps touching my arm and shoulder. *Keep your hands off me, buster.* And when I ask what flavor the ice cream is, before I can say the proverbial Jack Robinson he puts his spoon to my mouth so I can taste it.

*I wish it were Loren sitting next to me or someone to whom I was attracted.* Once when Loren and I were coming home from Europe we were upgraded to first class and drank champagne and giggled most of the trip. When I got tired, I just lay my head on his shoulder. I can't do that with this man.

"If there is anything you need while you're here in Hawaii, please call me," he says as he hands me his card at the end of the flight.

"So, did you call Mr. Hawaii?" Sue asks when I return home.

"No, why get entangled in a relationship that I know from the start is not right? But I did learn one thing from this experience."

"What's that?" Sue asks.

"I know it sounds trite, but I learned that you never know what's going to happen or when you might meet somebody. I never would have thought that, on my way to a solitary vacation, I would talk during the entire flight to an unknown man who sat next to me. Perhaps on future trips a man who can pass the penis test will sit down."

"You never know," Sue agrees. "Remember, we used to think that way when we were young, before I met Vic and you met Loren. Judy, I think you're getting younger."

I smile to myself at her supportive suggestion, then add, "But on a more serious note, I realize that dating means moving forward and leaving Loren behind. It's so painful to look forward to a new life and yet not want to let go of the old one."

"I can imagine," Sue responds in a warm voice, "but remember there is no time schedule, only your own."

"I know," I reply. "But sometimes I worry that my wish to hold on to Loren will interfere with my letting other men into my life. I can laugh about the penis test, which I honestly think has some validity, but it's just hard—" I giggle and add, "Not the penis, I mean this continuous bind I feel."

"Have faith in yourself," Sue responds, with laughter in her voice. "Your instincts have always been good; they won't let you down now. Gotta go, love ya."

⁓

The next week I stand in front of the condom display at the very same Rite Aide drugstore where I bought the spiral notebooks after Loren was diagnosed with cancer. *How did I get here? Why am I standing here?* My mind wanders. I am twelve years old, buying my first box of sanitary napkins, hidden in the middle of my basket that overflows with unneeded sundries—toothpaste, toothbrush, tissues, and witch hazel. At the checkout counter, I am hopeful that my neighborhood pharmacist doesn't notice my concealed item.

I wake up from my reverie to find myself staring at an enormous selection of condoms. Who knew that condoms range in price from $3.99 for the no frills variety to $33.99 for the genuine lambskin brand? *Okay, I can handle this. It's like any other shopping trip.* Drawing on my vast shopping experience, I focus on the middle price range. *Oh God, they come in sizes! How am I supposed to know the size if I've never seen it? Worse, they come ribbed for her delight, ticklers for his and her delight.* I think that buying my first house was easier than buying my first condoms and walk away.

I remember my father once telling me how impressed he was with the way Loren broadened my horizons. Well, I think, here's another example. If my husband had not died, I would not be standing here looking at condoms. When Loren and I met, in the mid 1970s, I told him my philosophy about sex: It was like shaking hands. You got it out of the way first, and then there was no anxiety about it. This assumed, of course, that there was a physical attraction and hope of a future relationship. Loren loved my philosophy, and since we had an instantaneous attraction to each other we did have sex our first night together and it was great then and thereafter. Loren was a gentle lover, always concerned about my pleasure as well as his own. Maybe it was my youth, or perhaps just the times, that allowed for such a free philosophy. In those days women only worried about getting pregnant, not about AIDS and other sexually transmitted diseases. Now, because Loren died I have to face all the uncertainty and anxiety, only this time it's more serious. But my experience on the airplane showed me what could happen, so the lyrics of Tom Lehrer's song "Be Prepared" keep going through my head.

I return to the Rite Aide the next day, peruse the assortment yet again, and, like a good businesswoman, go with a sure thing. Trojans—no worry about sizes, no inside and outside ticklers, three to a pack, medium priced. I'm pleased that I'm mature enough and don't have to buy ten unneeded items as a coverup. Nevertheless, I go to a cashier I don't know and pay for them. I feel both triumphant and sad. I got the condoms just in case; yet what if such a scenario occurs?

As I exit the drugstore, I think about the myth of Orpheus and Euridyice, in which Orpheus is told not to look back as he leads Eurydice from Hades or she will be dragged back to Hades. I wonder if I continue looking back to Loren too often, will I be dragged back to the past, unable to move forward?

# *11*

# Blending Memories

*Music, when soft voices die,*
*Vibrates in the memory;*
*Odors, when sweet violets sicken,*
*Live within the sense they quicken.*
*Rose leaves, when the rose is dead.*
*Are heaped for the beloved's bed;*
*And so thy thoughts, when thou art gone,*
*Love itself shall slumber on.*

*—Percy Bysshe Shelley*

"PERHAPS I SHOULD GO SOMEWHERE WE NEVER WENT," I SAY TO BEV during my weekly therapy session. "Then I can form new memories, just as we did when we moved here. Did I ever tell you Loren's philosophy about moving?"

"No, tell me," she replies.

"One night while we were discussing the pros and cons of moving, he took my hand in his and said, 'It will be good, Judy. We will make new memories. We'll be like an uprooted tree. The leaves will fall off, we'll put down new roots, and soon new leaves will grow.' It never occurred to me at the time that one of the trees, Loren, would die. Anyway, we did form new memories and also what I call blended memories—incorporating experiences, rituals, and friends from Washington, D.C., into our life here in San Diego. Maybe I can do that now, joining together the memories of my past with Loren and my new life as a widow."

"That's a good idea," she responds, with a smile. "Any thoughts on where you want to go?"

"I've looked at a lot of travel brochures over these past two years and nothing appealed to me. Maybe it was too soon. But last week I found a trip to Croatia that attracts me."

"What is it about that trip that draws you to it?" Bev asks as she shifts in her chair and extends a pointed foot toward me, a gesture I've learned to understand as emphasizing a point.

"Loren and I have never been to Croatia, so it would be all new for me. The descriptions and pictures of the Mediterranean Sea, and the surrounding ports and cities, are colorful and gorgeous. Also, ten days of the trip are on a schooner, and Loren and I talked about doing that."

I take a minute to reach over and grab a tissue to blot my now tearing eyes then continue, "But I'm scared. Although Loren's death made me feel like my leaves fell off, I am bare, and I don't know if I want to put on new leaves—make new memories to replace the old ones."

"What are you really afraid of, Judy?"

"That if I make enough new memories the old ones will be replaced—forgotten." *Will this ambivalence never end?* "I want to move forward into a new life, yet . . . It's so simple, I guess: I wish Loren were still alive. But he isn't."

"Although Loren may fade a bit from your everyday life, and he has to so you can live your life, he will always be part of you. He is part of who you are today," Bev reassures me.

"I know, but I still miss him."

"You always will," Bev concludes realistically.

On the drive home, I smile to myself, remembering how Loren used to call my car Annie Accord, and his car, which was a Jaguar, Dr. J. *If we can make cars into humans, why can't we make humans into cars?* These days I often feel like a magical car that goes forward and backward at the same time yet is not stuck, just constantly going from gear to gear. I experience conflicting motions, wondering if I should go to Croatia or if I should stay home. I push myself into forward gear and decide to go. Loren hated tours, but then he never had to travel alone. I conclude that this is a good way for me to start.

The next week I begin packing for the trip. I put carefully rolled-up yellow and orange T-shirts in my duffel bag, then take them out again. Indecisive, I think maybe I should stick with black and white, then shift again to colors. *What's wrong with me? I never have trouble packing.* I realize that my indecisiveness is not really about colors but about going on the trip. I'm still besieged with doubts and questions, even as I feel excited. How will it feel? Should I take Loren with me—his ashes—or go it alone? I pack some ashes.

Finally, I finish packing and call the airline.

"Sorry, ma'am, it's a full flight. I doubt very much that you will get an upgrade, even at the gate," says the gruff voice of the reservation lady. *So much for new memories. Clearly, as in the past, I don't have Loren's luck at getting upgrades.* I decide I have to get used to blended memories, permitting the old ones to be there yet also allowing new memories in, and not be frightened of either.

At the San Francisco airport, my eyes roam over the assembled masses in the waiting area. Some guy with a crew cut, who looks like one of the church proselytizers who appear at my door—very clean cut in a white open shirt, dark trousers, and polished shoes—catches my eye through his Elvis Costello glasses and smiles. Please not him, I silently incant as I glance at the stub in his hand and see that his seat assignment is 38E, while mine is 38D.

After boarding, I sit in my coveted aisle seat as Mr. Too Clean Cut takes the seat next to me and starts talking. I look at my book in an effort to ignore him, but I cannot comprehend anything because of his constant patter.

"Oh, excuse me," he says in an agitated voice, "perhaps I talk too much." I think perhaps Mr. White Shirt, Dark Trousers has some insight! I continue reading, or rather viewing, the page in front of me, but he continues to talk.

As a solution, I put on the earphones and connect them to the on-board music, knowing I don't have to listen to the music but that the earphones will provide another layer between him and me. I suddenly recall that Loren would sometimes put on his earphones, and wonder if he did that when I wanted to talk and he did not. *Does this count as blended memory?* This is going to be a long flight. I pop a Valium. Before I drift off to sleep, I get pissed at Loren once again. If he were with me, this would likely not have happened and we would have gotten the upgrade because of his higher frequent flyer status and be together. *Did I make a mistake? Can I handle this trip by myself?*

I disembark in Frankfurt and try to find the gate for Croatia Airlines. As I stand around waiting, I hear prayer. *I must be going nuts.* I'm ready to check myself into the nearest loony bin when my gaze falls on a group of about twenty religious men and women, reciting the rosary out loud, on a pilgrimage to Dubrovnik. I wonder if they can save me.

Then I turn around when I hear a voice saying, "Yes, I raced at Santa Rosa, Del Mar, and all the big ones," and see a rotund man, about three feet tall, earring in one ear, khaki shorts and striped T-shirt, giving out autographed pictures of when he was a jockey. I idly wonder if Loren is playing with me.

After another flight and taxi ride, I arrive at the hotel in Dubrovnik. The receptionist tells me about the rooftop swimming pool and gives me a key to my small but adequate room. Now I'm alone in an exquisite port city on the Adriatic that Loren would have loved. I wonder what he would do here upon our arrival and decide that he would look at his guidebook, identify some wonderful restaurants and churches, and off we would go. When we traveled, Loren was my personal tour guide; here I am on my own. *So, he's not here. I'm not helpless. I, too, can find a restaurant. Blend memories.* It occurs to me that I'm knitting the old and new memories together, but I don't have a specific pattern or any precise directions.

Once unpacked, I wander up a path that winds around the clear water. Couples lie on the rocks, absorbing the afternoon sun. I meander along the seaside, investigating cafés to find a nice spot for dinner overlooking the sea . . . at sunset . . . alone.

"Table for one, please," I respond to the hostess, holding my head up high and smiling to give myself courage.

"Would you like the buffet or the à la carte menu?" she asks as she seats me at a lovely table overlooking the rainbow-colored water, the special color of the sea that appears at dusk.

Loren hated buffets, except for the sumptuous breakfast buffets in some European hotels, where we would stuff food in my backpack for a picnic lunch. *Have to work on these blended memories.*

"I'll take the à la carte menu, thanks," I answer, and order shrimp scampi and the local house white wine. I remember that Loren always ordered the local wine when we traveled, saying it was usually very good and less expensive. *Okay, I did get here and order.*

"Do you want a glass or the bottle?" the waitress asks.

"I'll take the small bottle, please," I respond offhandedly. But when the wine arrives it is a full-size bottle. *Did I expect Loren to show up if I ordered enough for two?* The handsome busboy, who speaks no English, smiles as he places the .75 litre bottle of wine and the beautifully grilled scampi in front of me. I drink all of the perfectly chilled wine. I figure I earned it. I am here on my first solo trip and need fortification.

Afterward, I wobble back to the hotel and go to the bar. Loren always ended his meal with his favorite liqueur—a glass of Sambuca with three coffee beans, which he claimed represented health, happiness, and prosperity. I order a Sambuca and think to myself, Well, I have my health, I'm not worried about prosperity, and I'm working on happiness. I silently toast Loren and thank him for all the good times we had and for all he taught me. I realize that Bev was right—he will always be a part of me.

When I climb the stairs to my small room and open the door, I'm surprised Loren is not waiting for me. But in this state of constant movement, as the metaphorical car jerks forward and backward, I marvel at my expanding capabilities—being able to plan this trip to a new and unfamiliar place, enjoying a meal by myself at a lovely, romantic seaside café, and even having a more open mind about meeting new men. I look in the mirror and smile at my image, wondering what the future holds and if I will be a permanent widow.

Several days later the noon sun warms my face on the 135-foot schooner with eight other people—two couples who have been married fifty years and several single women. The boat, built in 1903, has a shiny white steel hull with deep blue trim, is double masted, and has three aft sails. Its name, *The Flying Dutchman*, implies magic, redemption, and love, as in the Wagner opera. Klass, the Dutch captain, is deeply tanned, sports a salt-and-pepper beard and mustache, and has an elfin twinkle in his deep blue eyes. He wears gray shorts, a baby blue T-shirt, and the requisite captain's cap as he stands at the helm, his strong hands on the massive brass wheel.

The royal blue of the Adriatic Sea surrounds us, with the smaller ancient islands of Croatia—Mijet, Korčula, and Hvar—on the starboard side. I look around at the beauty, breathe in the familiar salt air, and I'm flooded with sailing memories.

In 1977, Loren and I, along with two other couples, rented a boat in Eleuthera, an island paradise with miles of glistening white and pink sand. There was a huge storm, and we lost the dinghy. Loren and our friend Larry, in their bright red-orange rain gear, tried to steer the boat as the wind ripped around us. The three women were squawking with fear. After Larry ordered us to be quiet, we sat like three ducks in a row, in our yellow rain parkas. When the engine stopped, we each took a turn manually rotating it. Finally we reached our house in Eleuthera. The women flipped coins for the three rooms. Loren and I got a nice big room, away from the others, which provided privacy, and we unwound from the strain of the day by making passionate love.

*Will I ever have passionate sex again? It doesn't seem possible, but who knows.* I never thought I would have passionate sex ever until I met Loren. I will always treasure the memory of our lovemaking, and if at some time there is another man I will consider myself a very lucky woman.

A year later, we sailed to a deserted beach in the Exumas, a group of 365 cays and islands that stretch over twenty miles. The sand was white, with whole sand dollars everywhere, giving the effect of lace. Donna, Larry's wife, and I were in the galley fixing lunch when suddenly Loren and Larry stopped talking. I peeked through the hatch and immediately understood the reason for their silence. Another sailboat was anchoring next to us, but although that was not unusual, the method of anchoring was. A gorgeous young woman in her mid-twenties, with a long blonde braid cascading down her back and without a stitch of clothing on her beautiful bronzed body, carried the anchor to shore and placed it in the sand, as if transporting a sacred object. I half expected to hear someone yell out, "But look, the empress has no clothes," because indeed she did look regal. *Will I ever find new experiences to equal this one?* The answer to that, I realize, is yes, if I make them happen just as Loren and I did, and am open to such possibilities.

The next winter we anchored in the harbor of St. Martin. My job was to put down and pull up the anchor. Loren was at the helm. Tim, Loren's son, was with us. The night was dark, the harbor was crowded, the wind was howling, and the boat was rocking back and forth, so we decided we needed to leave that spot and anchor again elsewhere. But the anchor was stuck, and as the wind continued its baleful sound I pulled at the anchor with all my strength, but could not budge it. Recalling the bronzed empress who had no clothes, I quickly stripped and dove in, but being no empress I was grateful for the cover of night. After I discovered that the anchor was tangled with other anchors, I managed to free it and we anchored in a safer spot. Loren often teased me by calling me his "football-player wife" because of the muscled, broad shoulders I developed over the years of pulling anchors. *Will I ever find someone who can both admire a regal nude empress and still be proud of my quarterback shoulders and later my sags and wrinkles? Loren taught me to be proud of both my younger and older bodies.* I have no answer but to look forward to the future with hopes of the new memories it may hold.

A couple of months before we got married in 1988, Loren and I and Donna and Larry were on our thirty-two-foot sailboat, *The Driftwind*. We were returning to Florida from Bimini, a tiny island in the Bahamas. The weather was stormy, our boat was rocking, and we didn't know where we were. Donna and I, acknowledging that we were much less experienced sailors than the men, went below deck and hung up our hard-won cloaks of feminism, never doubting that our men would get us to safety.

Then Loren beckoned me up to the deck and said in a low whisper, "Judy, I don't want you to panic but go get the scissors because I think we might need to cut the rope and use the life raft."

"What do you mean?" I asked with terror in my voice.

"Just go get the scissors," Loren responded with a tone of urgency.

I went below deck and, trying to maintain my balance as the waves soared around us, located the scissors and secretively handed them to Loren. I wondered whether we would reach our destination safely, but we did. *Will I ever again be able to trust someone so completely with my life?* Perhaps I must trust myself since I am now the person completely in charge of my life.

Loren and I finally had to give up sailing after we realized we could no longer manage the boat by ourselves. During our last trip, we were in the Turks and Caicos, a big wind came up, and, although it was difficult to lower the sails, we finally did it and motored into the harbor. My assignment was to pick up the mooring line, which, even in calm weather, demands some degree of coordination. I was ready with the boat hook but missed. I continued a dance of trying and missing until I finally was able to grab it but could barely hold it in my hands. Loren was bruised all over, while I had rope burns on my hand. Luckily, someone came out on a motorboat to help us, and the experience made us realize that although we loved sailing we could no longer do it alone. We acknowledged the passage of time and decided we would find other activities more appropriate to being older. We would waltz, we rationalized, instead of dancing to the beat of a rock'n'roll band. *Will I ever find someone to waltz with me now?* It's true I'm older and less agile, but perhaps there is someone else out there who will waltz me through these later stages of life. And if not, I can surely dance by myself.

I awake from my reveries on *The Flying Dutchman* and realize that the sails are up and the motor off. I hear flute music and walk to the stern of the boat, where Klass, eyes closed, plays the flute. Mesmerized, I go to my cabin, get a handful of ashes, drop them in the Adriatic, and watch Loren blend with nature just as I hope my old and new memories will blend. And the sparkle of the ashes in the afternoon sun reminds me of the twinkling of Loren's eyes. The flute continues to play in the background, and as I again say good-bye to Loren, I contemplate a future without him. It occurs to me that I'm like a magician, and the old memories are the rabbit in my top hat. I don't need to let go of them; I can pull them out whenever I want to and relive them, keeping the magic of memories alive while also creating other tricks in the magic show.

I am surprised, and delighted, that I can have so much fun with a new group of people, in a new place—getting splashed and soaked on dinghy rides into the beautiful coastal towns, just as Loren and I did on many of our sailing trips; the spontaneous swimming in the Adriatic similar to past skinny dips in the Caribbean; the fabulous meals that Klass and his wife serve on board that remind me of Loren's gourmet shipboard meals; and sharing war stories with other women whose spouses have died. Now the memories of times with Loren do not seem to get in the way, but the fact that some of these new experiences feel vaguely familiar makes them less terrifying. They do blend into my old memories.

"Perhaps over time the old memories will become the roots to which the new memories are attached," I tell Bev when I return from the trip.

"Are you still concerned about being a permanent widow?" she asks.

I respond, "Not really. At some point during this trip I realized I could have fun by myself. I decided to stop worrying about the future and enjoy the gift of time."

# 12

# Honoring Loren's Legacy

*I suppose that every one of us hopes secretly for immortality;*
*to leave, I mean, a name behind him which will live forever in this world,*
*whatever he may be doing . . . in the next.*

—A. A. Milne

"Suz," I groan into the phone, "I have to do something about all of Loren's papers. They're his legacy. So last week, when I was in Palo Alto visiting Connie and the cemetery, I went to Stanford and talked to the archives librarians since Loren attended two years at Stanford Medical School before transferring to Harvard Medical School. I was so excited when they accepted his papers to be archived in the undergrad library. But now it just feels like another good-bye, and for sure I can't do this alone."

"I thought you said Roy was going to help you sort the papers. Isn't he an archives librarian of some sort?" Sue asks.

"No, but he was head of a college sociology department and spent many hours sorting other people's work so he's had experience with papers and knows what's valuable and what's not. His offer still stands, but once I call him I feel committed to the task. I'm not sure if I'm up to it yet." I think about all the overflowing file cabinets in Loren's office, and wonder if I can ever really sort through them, even with Roy's help. "When will this end? First his ashes, followed by his jewelry and clothing, and now his papers. I thought I got the car over the hump already, but there's always another challenge to face. I feel like I'm disassembling Loren piece by piece and there will be nothing left. I know I have to do it, but I still worry that I might forget about him," I reply.

"C'mon, Judy, you know that's not true. It may feel that way right now, but you know that Loren will always be a part of you."

"Bev said the same thing to me. I hoped that at some point I would stop feeling so sad," I answer.

"But you have. It's just each time you face a new challenge you feel like you're starting all over again. After the trip to Croatia, you sounded so hopeful—happy and proud that you had done that."

"I guess I naively thought I was through with my grieving, when in reality there are just fewer times that I miss Loren and feel sad. And now this. I feel so overwhelmed when I walk into his office and see it as he left it. You know me and magic. I guess I thought if I left it alone he would one day turn up in the chair."

"Yes, I do know you and magic," Sue replies, laughing. "You know that's not going to happen."

I try to force a laugh, but instead burst into tears.

"It's okay, Judy," Sue comforts me. "It's only a little more than two years. Maybe you are putting too much pressure on yourself."

"But when will it end? Once I call Roy, I have to stick with it, and there goes another piece of Loren. But then I also shared him with the world when he was alive, and his work is too important not to be made available to future researchers. In fact, I believe that the concept of Soteria is developing into a movement. In England there is already a Soteria Network, and Soteria Alaska is on the way. It's like Loren said just before he was diagnosed: 'Judy, I think it's going to happen. Soteria is catching on.'"

"That's great! Judy, you were always so proud of the work Loren did. Think of sorting the papers for the archives as supporting Loren in death as you always did in his lifetime."

I suddenly feel tired. Tired of being brave, tired of missing Loren, tired of feeling sad, tired of dealing with everything. "I know, but I can't support him forever. I need to continue with my life as well," I respond.

"But letting go of Loren is continuing with your life. You're clearing space not only in your house but perhaps in your heart as well. Besides, you don't have to give everything away. You can keep anything you want. It's great that you negotiated for Loren's papers to be archived at Stanford. What an honor for him and for you, too," Sue says with admiration in her voice.

"Thanks, best friend, but I hate going through all Loren's files. You hear such horror stories of finding unexpected papers," I continue.

"What do you think you'll find—love letters to an old girlfriend, a long lost illegitimate child?" Sue asks, her voice quiet and firm, as if soothing a child frightened by a bad dream. "Besides, that's why Roy will be there, not only to sort but to support you."

"I'll never be ready," I acknowledge to Sue and myself, "but I have to do it. Besides, I have a secret plan." I lower my voice to a conspiratorial tone that reflects my guilt. "It would be unfortunate to waste the space, so I think I will make his office into my writing room. Ever since I started journaling and then took writing classes after Loren died, I've found I love writing, both its intellectual aspect and the solitude required. That way I'll use it for writing just as Loren did and share the room with his ghost."

After saying good-bye to Sue, I go into Loren's office. I'm startled to realize that I've been avoiding this room since Loren died. I slowly scan the space, trying to deposit everything in my memory bank before it disappears. Then I focus more intently on one side of the room, where I see the oak desk that Loren used for writing or talking on the telephone to colleagues or clients; the green banker's lamp I bought for him; the pencil holder made out of a juice container covered with colored rope that Missy brought home from school when she was seven years old; and the wall filled with pictures of Loren, which he mischievously called "Homage to Myself." There are two charcoal caricatures, one done on the bridge in Prague and the other by a client, both capturing and blending the essence of his bad boy and professorial sides. There are also some wonderful photos, particularly the one I had made for his fiftieth birthday party. When I sent out invitations, I asked everyone to include a one-word description of Loren with their RSVP. I then enlarged a brilliant color photo of him, mounted it on a box frame, typed out the words in different fonts, cut them out into various shapes, and laminated them onto the picture. It shows Loren with his salt-and-pepper hair combed back, his blue eyes bright, and his wonderful smile surrounded by words like *mad hatter* (he always wore a hat), *concupiscent* (he definitely was lustful), *leprechaun* (a reference to his Irish heritage), *quixotic* (an allusion to Don Quixote, who was always tilting at windmills), *incorrigible*, and my contribution, *nonjudgmental*—to me, one of his most important attributes. I know I can't give this picture away as it holds too much history.

I shift my gaze to the other side of the room and see the familiar computer table with Loren's old computer, printer, and fax machine—"office central," as he called this part. Sometimes after work, I would come into his office, swivel the black chair in front of the computer to face him as he turned his tan upholstered chair around to face me, and we would have heart-to-heart conversations about anything troubling us, such as Loren's disappointment about any negative responses to his work and his continuing belief that his approach—that being with clients was much more important than medicating them—was not only viable but also humane.

I then turn my attention to the many tapes in the oak bookcase, all the material in the two huge file cabinets and the boxes on the floor. I bend over for a second and leaf through the boxes. My body jerks back up as if struck by an unseen object. I slowly count to ten and bend down again so my eyes are level with the manila folders, which I see are sorted by date and subject, as if Loren knew someone would be looking through them later. Is it possible, I wonder, that Loren organized some of this material before he died? After all, he did know he was going to die. *His first words to me were "This is a death sentence."* It's all too difficult to assimilate. I put my head in my hands, close my eyes, and sob. After ten minutes, I go to the sink and splash cold water on my face and call Roy.

"Okay, I'm as ready as I'm gonna be. Let's start on the papers," I say with more enthusiasm than I really feel, like making a needed but unwanted doctor's appointment. "You know I really don't want to do this, but I do need to get started."

"How about Thursday from two to four?" he suggests.

"Thursday's good. Bring lots of tissues," I reply.

I wait for Thursday in a limbo of ambivalence, both dreading initiating the process of sorting the papers and eager to get it over with. Again I am like a car—moving forward, going backward. I also have mixed feelings about actually seeing Loren's papers, somewhat like a voyeur but also like an archaeologist preserving information for future generations.

Thursday arrives, and I try to figure out what to wear for this task. *Who am I getting dressed for? Certainly not Roy. He's a nice guy, but he lives with Connie and this is not a date. Loren?* Judy, I firmly tell myself, get real.

At exactly two o'clock, Roy arrives, smiling, in a blue-checked work shirt and jeans. He gives me a bear hug, smoothes his gray hair, and we walk back to the office.

"Where should we start?" I practically whine, while standing in the middle of the room, arms open in a questioning stance, feeling like a child being asked to clean up her toys.

"Let's start with the boxes on the floor," Roy says, as he plops in Loren's chair. *Get out of that chair. It's Loren's chair; he should be there.* Before I can start I pause, having to admit to myself that Loren will never again be in that chair, never again use this office.

Then I take deep breath and say, "Okay, let's begin. I'll hand a file to you, and I'll take one for myself." If I have questions, I'll ask you. But Roy, in addition to this being a difficult task, what if we find something I should never know about?"

"Judy, you've been seeing too many movies," Roy replies, putting his hand out for a file. His calm voice and demeanor make the process less frightening.

Every week for about two months Roy comes over on Thursday afternoons. We look at papers, destroy tapes, and organize Loren's legacy. It turns out to be both a difficult and enjoyable task. Although while experiencing pain at facing so many reminders of Loren, I also am pleasantly surprised to discover some fascinating and important documentation that reveals to me more about aspects of Loren that I loved. I find the correspondence between Loren and R.D. Laing, or Ronnie, as Loren called him, well-known radical psychiatrist and mentor to Loren. I had known they were friends but hadn't realized the extent of their friendship and correspondence. I have to smile when I remember the first time I met Laing. It was early in my relationship with Loren, and I flew to England, where Loren was presenting a paper at the Philadelphia Association, a group formed to discuss the theories of Laing. After the meeting and dinner, we went to a party at Laing's house. Following a couple of hours of drinking, everyone was passed out or sleeping on the floor except for Laing, who was playing the piano, and me. He stopped playing, looked at me over his half glasses and said in his Glaswegian brogue, "I would like to come on your eyelids." I was horrified, woke Loren up, and said either we leave the party immediately or I am going straight to the airport and returning home. Loren laughed, said I should be flattered, calmed me down with a gentle arm around my shoulders, and we left the party. It's hard to feel sad with such a colorful memory, except in acknowledging there will be no more experiences like that.

When I also discover Loren's thirty-year correspondence with Manfred Bleuler, the famous Swiss psychiatrist, in which they bemoan the biological leanings of psychiatry and Bleuler is especially supportive of Loren's work, I'm glad. I liked Freddie, as Loren called him when I first met him at Loren's house. We had just finished playing tennis, and Loren invited me over to meet Freddie. I had heard and read a lot about Bleuler but never expected to meet him, and not while wearing my sweaty tennis outfit while he was formally dressed in a three-piece pin-striped suit. After that, whenever we went to Switzerland we visited him. The bond between Freddie and Loren remained a cross between that of colleagues and father-son.

Every once in a while Roy laughs as he reads something to me that Loren wrote in a letter, and for those few minutes Loren is again in this office.

"I told you I was afraid I would find something in his papers that would surprise me," I tell Sue one Sunday.

"Told me what would happen, Judy?" she asks, sounding confused. "What? Loren has a long lost son and you now have four stepchildren instead of three?"

"This is not funny; this is serious," I reply.

"So don't keep me in suspense," Sue urges. I grab an emery board from the container on my desk and start filing my nails as we talk, something I do when I'm anxious.

"Guess what the title of the first paper Loren ever wrote was, in 1960? 'Carcinoma of the Liver and Post Necrotic Cirrhosis: Report of a Case Review of Carcinomas of the Liver Seen at Stanford 1919–1959.'"

"So?" Sue responds, perplexed.

"Loren died of liver cancer and he drank. He knew the consequences and he didn't stop. It makes me really angry with him, especially when I can't talk to him about it," I reply.

"Judy, you loved Loren for who he was, and you know he always enjoyed good wine and vodka. Do you think it would have changed anything?"

"No," I concede in defeat. "But it sure is ironic."

"Yes, it is. Have you finished going through everything now?"

"Just about. It's been a good process. We've both laughed and cried. I have been reminded of how proud I am of Loren's work, his ongoing disputes with the establishment, and his persistence and belief in himself. And I'm also proud of myself for supporting him all those years and for making it possible for others to access his legacy of papers, books, and correspondence. Now I have to get all this stuff up to Stanford. It sounds simple, but it feels like another huge task."

"You'll do it when it feels right," Sue says and then reminds me of all that I have accomplished.

Now that everything is sorted, I need to bring the papers to Maggie, the archivist at Stanford University. I go to Office Depot and bring home bank boxes in which to put Loren's papers—paper coffins, I think morbidly. I solemnly place the organized papers into eight somber dark cardboard boxes and label them MOSHER #1 through MOSHER #8, impressed with the breadth of his work.

Maggie tells me that I can send the boxes parcel post, but that feels impersonal—and too fast. I need to drive the boxes to Stanford, experiencing the entire process of letting go.

I decide to drive a rental car one way to Palo Alto and then fly back. It even seems important to choose the correct rental car for this solemn procession. I wonder whether I should get a black limousine, a BMW convertible (Loren loved his Beemer), or a Hummer? I think about asking for the economy size, but that doesn't feel right for this significant journey, and I decide to take the next size up from economy. The next day we're off — me driving, Loren in bank boxes — in a silver gray car. It feels like a funeral procession, taking Loren's papers to a far away, probably dark place. Despite my morbid thoughts, I continue to be pleased that Loren's legacy will be available to the world.

I have never driven the eight-hour trip from San Diego to northern California by myself and worry that I might not have the stamina to attain my goal of making it in one day or might get lost. Loren and I always shared driving when we went on car trips. I made sandwiches for us, and we took along wine and water for a portable picnic. When we moved to San Diego from Washington, D.C., also an emotionally difficult trip, we had cocktail hour in the car, nibbling on delicacies like cheese on crackers and sipping small amounts of wine.

The year before Loren died we made this same trip, but we were on our way to tour the California parks. I remember Loren giggling when he noticed that most of the other cars were "all filled up with old people, just like us, trying to get a start on the summer traffic, and all in the same silver gray-colored cars." But I'm on my own for this adventure. I try to focus on the purpose of the journey, feeling sad but also glad that I am preserving Loren's legacy. Before I left I googled Loren on impulse and was astounded at the number of citations. Now one more will be added, the entirety of his works available through the Stanford University computer system — Loren's professional legacy. His personal legacy of exciting experiences and intimate moments will remain in my own inner archives.

"So there I was," I tell Connie when I arrive safely in Palo Alto, "on the road with boxes of Loren's writings and correspondence and could feel his presence through his words. Once I got through the Los Angeles maze I relaxed a little more and noticed the beautiful surroundings."

"It's a pretty drive after that," she interrupts. We are sitting around the round oak table where we sat the night Loren and I returned from consultations at Stanford and UCSF. Connie wears her usual black turtleneck jersey and black pants, perfectly accented by a green jade necklace and bracelet, and with her gray hair tucked behind her ears in a neat pageboy.

"Yes, but I felt so sad when I passed through the fields of California blooming with purple lupine and orange and yellow wildflowers and I remembered the trip Loren and I took several years ago. Now we won't ever have any car trips again," I say, gulping my Chardonnay because I'm overwhelmed with the enormity of what I am doing.

"Loren's legacy is loaded with so much meaning. Of course, I know he is dead, but putting his papers in an archive is such a stark reminder," I continue.

"Yes it is. Did you play any music, something else to focus on?" Connie asks.

"Yes, I played music but it only stirred up more memories: Classical Chill, *Hair*, *Camelot*, Beatles, and Grateful Dead—all Loren's favorites, especially the Beatles and the Grateful Dead. Actually he didn't like musicals, so *Hair* and *Camelot* were for me. My emotions were really stirred up when 'Here Comes the Sun' came on, which he loved to play on those nights when we were high and roamed through the house munching on whatever was available, or even later at night when I sat on the ledge of the kitchen sink and watched him concoct some soup that would taste wonderful the next day. And the Grateful Dead—well, you know his friend was their lawyer so we went to almost all their concerts. The first time we went I was so stoned I couldn't find the stage," I say, giggling despite my sadness.

"But you got here safely. I admire you," Connie says, supportively.

"Thanks. I made my way across the state driving and crying. Even Bakersfield, with its flat dry land and thousands of cows, evoked memories. It was outside of Bakersfield, on the return of our state parks trip, where we enjoyed a fabulous gourmet meal at an elegant restaurant in the middle of nowhere. They even gave us menus with our names printed on them.

"As I passed Bakersfield I had to smile when I remembered Loren saying that the temperature in Bakersfield was higher than the cost of the hotel rooms. He did have a great sense of humor. I also recalled how much I loved it when Loren would sometimes drive with one hand on the steering wheel and one hand on my thigh, making me feel safe and protected. The memories made me feel sad, but they also made me smile as I remembered the life we had together. I cried as I listened to *Camelot* and heard the line 'Don't let it be forgot, that once there was a spot, for one brief shining moment that was known as Camelot.' I also had my shining moments with Loren and miss them." *Will I ever find another Camelot?* "For a second, I wondered whether we would have spent our time differently if we had known how limited it was. But I don't think so. As you know, Loren was always reminding me that 'this is not a dress rehearsal.' I feel fortunate that we never put anything off until 'retirement' or some later point."

Connie fills my wine glass, takes out some blue cheese from the refrigerator, grabs some crackers, and puts it all on the table.

"So many thoughts raced through my head as I drove on and on," I continue after cutting some cheese and popping it in my mouth. "Seeing Loren for the first time; Missy asking Loren if he loves her as much as me, and his wonderful answer, 'I love you differently'; Loren's following me home after I went through a red light to ask if I was okay; delightful orgasms; my dad asking Loren how his family felt about having a Jew in the family and Loren's quick response asking my dad how he felt about having a 'goy' in the family. Then, near the end of the trip, I suddenly had the insight that I was taking Loren home — since he was born in Monterey, grew up in Marin County, and graduated from Stanford — and that taking him home was right."

"Judy, you are an amazing woman. Loren was so lucky to find you," says Connie, with tears in her eyes.

Then we decide to go to bed to get ready for tomorrow when Connie will accompany me to deliver the boxes. I call up Loren's fraternity brother, Guy, and ask him if he would like to join us, and we plan to meet at a specific parking lot at eleven o'clock.

The next morning the regal sounds of Connie's grandfather clock seem an appropriate start to honor Loren and his legacy. I feel burdened with sadness, but Connie and Guy will be with me and somehow I know we will laugh.

I decide to wear black today, as Connie always does. It's a day to celebrate but also to commemorate. I transfer the boxes from the trunk of my car into the trunk of Connie's black Lexus, taking a picture each time I add a box, a visual diary of saying good-bye. At the assigned parking lot, Guy is waiting, wearing his usual green gray corduroy slacks and a checked shirt with a baggy sweater over it. He has been battling a variety of cancers in the last five years, and when Loren and I visited him in Stanford Hospital we thought he was going to die. The irony is that he survived while Loren died, and now we are taking Loren's legacy to be archived.

"What now?" he asks, as we get into Connie's car. He is uncomfortable and does not look me in the eye.

"We go to the back of the library and call Maggie. After that we will scatter some ashes, perhaps around your old fraternity house."

"Funny," Guy says. "I was thinking about Loren's professional legacy, and I had to smile when I thought about Loren's legacy to the fraternity house. He was the brain amongst all the jocks, but he sure kept up with all the partying. He was a hasher in the girls' dorm, and I always wanted to ask him if he did that just so he could be the first one to meet all the incoming coeds." We all laugh at the memory.

When we reach the loading dock, I call Maggie and she comes out, a petite brunette, with a welcoming smile, dressed as a college coed with a longish black skirt, nice shirt, and flat shoes. "Let me get a dolly, and we can unload them onto it and take them upstairs," she says. It is a quick, efficient transfer with no time for feeling. She shows us where Loren's legacy is for the moment and explains the process, saying, "When all the boxes are sorted and catalogued, the catalog will be sent to you, Judy, to check over, and then it will be put on the university computer, which is linked to universities around the world. Anyone who wants to pursue Loren's work will be able to access it and come here to look at any papers." She then asks me to sign a deed of gift to show that I'm now giving these papers to the university.

For a moment I wonder what would happen if I changed my mind. But then I remember how good it felt to give David Lee Loren's ring, to share the joy of Loren. And this time I am sharing Loren with many others who might want to learn about his work and his philosophy.

I take a moment to silently honor Loren and also to honor myself for this accomplishment, then solemnly sign the papers as I brush tears away from my eyes. I hope no one sees that, but when Connie puts her arm around me I know I have not been successful. *How many more times will I have to say good-bye to Loren?* Finally, I realize I am actually caring for him by sharing this legacy.

# 13
# Quantifying Grief

*There is no pain so great as the memory of joy in present grief.*

*—Aeschylus*

"How do you quantify grief?" I ask Sue early one Sunday morning. I'm still wearing my "Chicks Are Cool" pajamas with little yellow chickadees on them, which I bought because they make me smile when I go to bed alone.

"It's nine o'clock in the morning, Judy—that means it's six o'clock in San Diego. What are you doing up so early, and what do you mean?" Sue mumbles.

"I've been wondering about peoples' responses to grief, and there are a couple of concepts that I think are really significant, such as quantifying grief. I'm struggling to clarify it so I can write about it, or just as a way of helping future clients."

"How's the weather there?" Sue asks. "I'm not dodging your question, just thinking that if it's a nice day you can go to the beach and maybe clear your head. Sometimes that helps."

"Good idea," I interject, "but you still didn't answer my question."

I quietly open the pantry closet, take out a tall container of vitamins, and start placing my morning pills on a white napkin when the container falls to the floor.

"What's that noise?" Sue asks. "Do you have someone playing the cymbals in your house?"

"No," I say laughing, "my vitamin container just smashed on the floor, scattering hundreds of mustard-colored, pink, and white pills all over the marbled tile floor. It looks like someone just threw a thousand pieces of a jigsaw puzzle onto it. But that reflects how I feel this morning; I have many pieces of this puzzle I call quantifying grief but can't seem to put them all together."

"Tell me what you mean by quantifying grief," Sue asks.

"For example, when my father died, people often asked me how old he was. When I said eighty-two, the response would invariably be, 'Well, he had a good life.' That really upset me, as though the fact that he had a long life should lessen my grief. Were they implying that if he died when he was younger my grief would be more because of the years I never had with him or because his life was shortened?"

"Okay, I think I know what you mean. It's an interesting concept," Sue remarks. "I just remembered that another friend had the same experience when her father died at age eighty-five. She said people kept asking her how old he was and then said, 'That's not bad,' as though his age should have negated her sorrow somehow. Go to the beach and think about it some more. Maybe you'll get more clarity. Then call me later and let me know how you make out. Love ya," Sue says, concluding our conversation.

I like the idea of going to the beach to reflect on the concept. First I fix scrambled eggs with Parmesan cheese and dill, a breakfast I've perfected since Loren died and I have had to do my own cooking. By ten o'clock I get into my black bathing suit, put on a red and orange T-shirt from Split, Croatia, grab a beach chair, and drive to the beach.

Fifteen minutes later I'm at the beach, again contemplating the concept of quantifying grief. *Can its effect and duration be measured in minutes and hours? Months or years? Does it gradually diminish over time according to a specific formula? Or is grief an uncontrollable and immeasurable feeling that, once it has us in its grip, we must endure for an indeterminate amount of time? King Arthur, after all, mourned "one brief shining moment."*

Another aspect of grief is that practice does not make it perfect. I realize, for example, that my father's death did not prepare me for Loren's death, despite the fact that over the years the pain of losing my father gradually receded. Nevertheless, having become accustomed to the death of my father did not help me in any way face Loren's death. Unlike job interviews, where experience helps, with Loren's death I had to start from the bottom again, and people asked the same sort of questions, implying that length of a life or quality of a relationship somehow made the death easier to bear.

"How long have you been married?" several people asked me after Loren died, as if the length of our marriage determined the depth of my grief.

"We were formally married for sixteen years," I would say between clenched teeth.

"Oh," was the usual unemotional response.

"We lived together for twenty-two years," I would explain.

"Oh?" was often the answer, in a tone that showed a little emotion.

"And we knew each other for thirty years," I would add, as if upping the ante. It wasn't until then that I sensed some sympathy, as if they portioned out sympathy according to length of time couples had been together.

*Would I miss Loren less if we had spent less time together? Or more if he had died many years later? Am I mourning the years we had or the years we lost?* Surely it is the intensity of the relationship, not its duration, which determines the depth of grief, I conclude.

I realize that the grief I feel indeed seems to be magnified by the intensity and unique qualities of our relationship. As I listen to opera on my iPod to get even greater clarity, an aria from Puccini's *Turandot* pierces my consciousness. I close my eyes and smile as I see Loren at the opera wearing his fancy black handmade Italian tuxedo and staid British high-neck white tuxedo shirt, any idea of somberness set to rest by the contrast of a flamboyant bright red cummerbund and vest covered with brightly colored birds. Loren called the opera "circus for adults." This reflected a fundamental aspect of Loren's character: he liked fun that was tinged with elegance and adventure.

I smile again as I remember another experience tinged with elegance and adventure. To celebrate my parents' fiftieth anniversary, Loren had insisted that we take them to the opulent Rainbow Room, the restaurant at the top of the Rockefeller Center Building with a spectacular view of the New York City skyline. But Loren was flying into New York from Italy on the very day of the celebration, and for the plan to succeed every one of his connections had to be perfect. I held his tuxedo and my breath in a hotel room, hoping that he would arrive on time, and miraculously he did. He changed into his tuxedo, we stepped into the waiting limo, picked up my parents, and arrived at the Rainbow Room at the exact time of our reservation.

I also realize, however, that the intensity of my grief reflects the depth of our mutual support. As phrases from *The Messiah*, the next selection on the iPod, interrupt my reverie, I remember how Loren, when discouraged because of being disparaged and marginalized by his psychiatric colleagues for his belief system, would blast *The Messiah* and tears would fill his azure blue eyes. It was my cue to sit with him and wait until he was ready to talk. Similarly, when I was distressed about my mother's decline and possible death, I, too, played *The Messiah* and Loren would sit with me until I was ready to talk. This became an unspoken symbol of our mutual support. *What adds more to my grief—our history of fun and adventure or our mutual support?*

I further realize that the depth of my grief reflects the fact that Loren taught me how to live life to the fullest, a lesson that even after his death I follow. Together we witnessed some of nature's most powerful manifestations. For my fiftieth birthday, which was also Passover and our fourth anniversary, Loren surprised me with a trip to Maui. One morning we got up early to walk around the dormant volcano, Haleakula. We watched the sun go from a peek of light to its full brightness as we walked over solidified black lava that was hundreds of years old.

On that same trip, but on the Big Island of Hawaii, we flew by helicopter over the volcano Kilauea. I am terrified of heights, and Loren had his hand protectively on my thigh the whole time. When we were over the volcano, Loren persuaded me to look down, and I was both stunned and petrified. I felt like I was looking into the soul of God, or the devil. I could feel the heat of the orange-red inferno below and was certain some invisible spirit was churning up this cauldron. *How do I quantify the importance of such magical moments in relation to the depth of grief?*

I always thought of our relationship as magical, although there were parts of our life that were not. For example, there was the time I broke up with Loren after we had been dating for about a year. He continued to ask me out, and the lure of his charm constantly tempted me. Finally, after six months of being pulled back, but afraid of being hurt, I called up my Aunt Bea, a tiny slip of a woman, barely five feet tall and weighing about ninety pounds.

"If you really love someone and they hurt you but want to see you, what do you do?" I asked her, more like a child than the woman I was.

"Do you love him?" she asked back.

"Yes."

"Then go back and see what happens," she advised.

I did, and my relationship with Loren became the happiest one of my life. *Should those six months of unhappiness be subtracted from the grief I felt at his death?* I picture a blackboard with equations written helter-skelter in white chalk, such as:

> Years married − Time separated by work or travel = Intensity of grief

or

> Years of living together + Years of marriage − Times not talking = Extent of grief

or, in deference to the high school equation Rate x Time = Distance

> Age x Percentage of time making love = Grief

Ultimately, I realize all such hypothesizing is preposterous since grief cannot be measured but is a deep emotion felt uniquely by each person.

After several hours, I leave the beach and return home. I brush the sand off my body and jump in the shower to cool off. Before calling Sue I put on my jean shorts and a white T-shirt. "Nice legs," I can hear Loren say, as he often did. *But no more.*

I call Sue, who asks, "Did you come to any conclusions?"

"I decided that each person mourns according to their own style. You don't have to tell me, I know my style is intense. But I realized that there really is no way to quantify grief; it's unique to each person and may or may not reflect the relationship to the deceased. Emotions are ephemeral and capricious. They cannot be measured. I think the people who ask how long someone lived, how old the person was, or the length of the marriage or relationship are stupid, inept, or just don't know what to say to someone who is mourning. I admit I've caught myself saying the same things, but now I try to keep in mind that King Arthur's one shining moment was probably as important for him as my thirty years with Loren were for me."

"Sounds like you did a lot of thinking."

"Yes, and I conceptualized another thought as well. It has to do with the difference between people who want to share your grief and people who just want your grief."

"Now you're getting subtle on me. Explain," Sue urges.

"I know it sounds like a subtle difference, but I thought about all the people who have been wonderful and helped me, like you, as opposed to others who just wanted to hear more about my grief, like they were watching some tragic movie. For example, when about a year after Loren died someone who just found out called me, upset, and kept asking for details, I felt like she was taking my grief away and making it her own, a feeling I didn't like. It was as if this person wanted the experience to be hers."

"You may be on to something, don't give up. Sorry, Vic's calling, time to go. Love ya."

I hang up the phone and plop down in the Eames chair, Loren's chair, and ponder how someone steals grief. I try to let my mind roam the highway of the last few years, looking for more examples and explanations of my concept.

For one thing, I feel a kind of selfishness from people who want to steal my grief in contrast to members of the bereavement group who all genuinely shared grief. At the memorial service there was another friend who wanted to know all about how Loren died, and when I told her, I felt I didn't get any return on my investment of emotions. And I have a couple of widow friends who, even though they have their own grief, want mine. It's like they want to hear my experience so they can compare it to theirs—that's not sharing, it's taking for purposes of one's own needs.

In this context, I picture the lawyers called ambulance chasers who don't care about the people involved in accidents but only want their business so they can make money. I decide there's a group of people who are grief chasers, who don't care about the person grieving but only want the gory details of the person's experience so they can be empowered and gossip or be part of the drama. The word *Schadenfreude*—gaining happiness from the misfortunes of others—seems to reflect the either conscious or unconscious motivation of grief chasers. They don't care about me personally but seem to enjoy the fact that I am miserable, which explains their quest for more and more details and the lack of sympathy that I experience when interacting with them.

Finally, I realize that I own my grief. And although it ebbs and flows, it is neither a murky, stagnant pool filled with dead flies nor is it a dangerous riptide that can kill. It cannot be measured, nor can it be taken away from me. It is my personal place where I keep Loren. My grief reminds me of our love, and our love reminds me that I am alive and perhaps even have the capacity to love again.

# *14*

# Tincture of Time

*Hope, like the gleaming taper's light,*
*Adorns and cheers our way;*
*And still, as darker grows the night,*
*Emits a brighter ray.*

—*Oliver Goldsmith*

"WHAT ARE YOU DOING TODAY?" SUE ASKS. "MIGHT BE A TOUGH DAY."

It's September 3, 2006, which would have been Loren's seventy-third birthday—over two years since his death.

"Unless Loren magically appears, there will be no birthday celebration. You're right—it may be difficult. The kids and I all agree it's a hard day but not as bad as last year. Some of the shock has worn off, and perhaps we are slowly getting used to the situation. But on the bright side, I invited my friend Carla over for dinner, the woman whose husband died two years before Loren."

"What're you making for dinner? I'm sure you have quite a repertoire by now," Sue asks.

"Sushi, chicken wings, and watermelon—the ultimate culturally diverse meal. Who would have thought that after Loren died I would actually be planning successful meals not only for myself but also for company. You know I always cooked an occasional special meal, but now it is almost routine to make nightly dinners for myself and for company as well.

"I'm making a simple meal because I didn't want to have any leftovers since tomorrow night I fly off to Rome for ten days. I'm staying in the same hotel as last year when I brought ashes to Venice, which seems like light years away. To paraphrase the song, What a difference a year makes. Now I'm ready to have fun. I'll call you when I get back. Ciao."

"Showoff. Even I know that Italian word. Don't forget to take condoms. Love ya," Sue replies.

After hanging up the phone, I realize that while I feel saddened by yet another anniversary date, I'm really looking forward to this trip. I learned on the trip to Croatia that I can successfully travel alone, but still that was mostly with a tour group. This time I'm going solo. I love Rome, I love the Italians, and I might even meet some gorgeous *signor* who will sweep me off my feet—if only for a little while. *Are those sexual stirrings I feel?* Part of me feels guilty, like I'm sneaking off to have a good time, but why not? *C'mon, Judy, missing Loren and having a good time without him are not mutually exclusive. Lighten up.*

I go into the bedroom and lay out my clothes. I experience no hesitation this time, and I don't even care about being upgraded. I just want to get there, eat pasta and pizza, drink good wine, visit with my friend Roberto and his family, and see if any sinsemilla grew in the soil where he placed Loren's ashes last year.

When it is time to make dinner, I arrange the sushi on a colorful Italian ceramic plate, wash off the chicken wings, stick them in the bowl of Wishbone Italian dressing to marinate, cut up the watermelon, and set the table. I gaze at the bright orange placemats, yellow napkins, and the new white dishes. *The table looks colorful like the old days, but Loren hasn't seen the new dishes. Guess the old days are really gone, as they have to be to make room for new experiences and the rest of my life still ahead.*

The sound of the telephone interrupts my musings, and I assume it's Carla calling to say she will be late. But Randy asks breathlessly, "Did ya hear?" Words foreboding of disaster.

"No, what happened?" I barely squeak out, afraid to hear the answer.

"Dwayne was murdered by a patient today," Randy reports. "I wanted to tell you, since Loren was Dwayne's mentor, and you guys were always good friends."

My voice falters. "I can't fathom it." *I don't want to talk about death. I am going on a holiday.*

I hear the single chime of the doorbell.

"Have to go and tomorrow I'm off to Rome so I'll try to call you from the airport or when I get back. Thanks for calling," I say.

The dinner with Carla is good, but I can't stop thinking about Dwayne's death. The last time I saw him was about five years ago during one of our visits to Washington, D.C., when we met him and his wife, Fran, at a local bar. We laughed and caught up with each other's lives, both professional and personal, then went back to their house afterward, where Dwayne softly played the guitar. Why would someone murder this gentle man, I wonder.

"That's horrible," Carla says when I tell her what happened. "In a funny way you and I were lucky, Judy. At least we had time to say good-bye to our husbands."

"Yes, as awful as their deaths were, we were somewhat prepared, although I don't think anyone is really prepared for the finality of death. Yet I do believe that kind of closure makes it easier to move forward, and we are moving forward in our respective lives."

She gets me back on track by asking about my trip, reminding me about condoms.

I shyly share with her my awareness of some sexual stirrings and then continue, "I don't know if I ever told you that Loren and I had private pet names for our genitals—Charles and Armanda."

"Where'd you come up with those names? Sounds like the royalty of England," Carla responds with glee in her voice.

"I don't remember where those names came from. We used to send each other cards—To: Armanda, Love Charles, or the opposite—with little gifts. On my sixty-second birthday, Charles gave Armanda a lovely battery-operated penis-shaped dildo. We laughed about it, and I put it in my drawer, under lots of stuff. I found it about a week ago, coincidentally with the beginnings of my awareness of new sexual feelings. Aha, I thought, why not use this to pleasure myself—a little crazy, but since it was from Charles, well, you

can imagine the rest. But the most interesting thing is that sometimes when
I sleep on my side I hold on to it, as though I were sleeping with Loren. Often when we fell asleep I was holding his penis, so this feels totally natural,
a transitional object that makes me feel good, like a child's favorite doll or
teddy bear. So, am I nuts?"

"No," Carla says, "maybe just more creative than some. We single women
have to figure out ways to fill those gaps. I told you that since I got the small
new dog, he sleeps with me and farts and snores just like Ronald did. By the
way, are those condoms still good?"

"Funny you should ask. I didn't even know condoms had expiration dates
until I asked one of my younger friends. The first batch I bought expired, but
I got a second package for this trip, just in case."

At the end of the evening, Carla says, as we hug good-bye, "Have a
great time."

"I plan to," I respond, more confidently than ever before.

I get into bed then realize I forgot to put the condoms in my luggage.
When I open the top drawer, I laugh, seeing they are right next to Loren's
ashes. I never thought that I would find the sight of ashes next to condoms
comical, but then I never thought of a future after Loren died.

Once in bed again I can't sleep because I am excited about the trip and
also thinking about Dwayne's death. I resort to my old trick of counting
backwards from some random monetary number, $1,245.50.

As I wake up, I again think about Dwayne and try to comprehend his
death. All day I discipline my mind, unruly as a child in kindergarten class, to
stay focused on packing, but I still think about Dwayne's death, and his wife
Fran's new role as widow. I want to tell her that life will get better, but I know
she will not believe me, just as I never would have believed it if someone had
said this to me when Loren first died. But life has gotten better. As much
pain as I feel now, it is not the searing pain of two years ago. Sure there are
reminders and sadness but not the constant minute-by-minute memories that
remind me of Loren's death and absence. I'm ashamed that I feel glad about
having passed the initial numbness and horror of Loren's death. Four months
was not a lot of time to acclimate to Loren's upcoming death, but to have no
notice at all and have a husband murdered must be even worse.

I push my anxiety aside, as if it were a huge boulder blocking my path, and call Fran, the new widow, feeling that it's my job to initiate her into the sorority of widows.

"Hi, who's this?" I ask when someone answers the phone at Fran's house.

"Fran's brother. Who's this?"

"This is Judy Schreiber-Mosher, a friend of Fran's. Can I speak to her?"

"Sorry Judy, Fran's with the rabbi right now. She can't speak to you." I feel relieved and guilty that I feel relieved.

Then I hear Fran's soft voice in the background. "I want to talk to her."

Despite all my practice, I don't know what to say. I want to make this experience easier for her and try to remember what was helpful to me.

She says hello without any emotion.

"God, Fran, I am so sorry. How awful," I say.

"Yeah, it's horrible," Fran replies.

How can I tell Fran that at some point she will enjoy life again — laugh, travel, and perhaps even have sexual feelings? I can't, although as I think about my journey through grief, I realize that is exactly what happened. It suddenly occurs to me, that I feel hopeful about my unknown future.

"Listen, I know that there will be lots of people there for a while. I want to come and spend some time with you, but later after everyone leaves. I'm on my way to the airport. I'll call you when I get back from Europe," I say.

"Thanks for calling, Judy. I love you," she replies, her voice sounding hollow like that of a child frightened by a bad dream. I wish I could hug her tiny body and make it all go away. But even I, with all my thoughts of magic and experience with therapy, know that only time will make it easier for her.

When I get to the airport, I can't help but think about that time more than two years ago when I walked off the plane, numb with grief as Fran is now, carrying Loren's ashes and entering an unknown phase of life. Two years has made such a difference — "tincture of time" has indeed helped in my healing. Of course, when Loren said that phrase to me it was often in relation to my distress about something my mother said, or even some slight rash or bump on my body. He could never have known that this nugget of wisdom would help me face his own death and my grief.

I feel the need to connect to friends, and decide to use my layover time in Washington, D.C., to make some calls. "I'm in the airport," I tell Carol. "Did you hear about Dwayne?" Carol and I met in 1974 when we both worked at the National Institute of Mental Health. It was before I met Loren and before she married Will, also a psychiatrist. I picture her tiny frame and long brown hair, now gray.

"Yes, it's horrible. In fact, we're going over there soon," Carol replies. "But how're you doing, Judy? It's about two years since Loren died, I figure."

"Yes, a little over two years. I'm on my way to Rome." As we talk I flip through the local Washington paper to see if there are any articles about the murder. I find one and just stare at it until I realize Carol is still talking to me.

"You sound good, Judy, and strong," she says.

Although I know she doesn't intend to make me feel guilty and is only surprised that I'm moving on, nevertheless I still feel like I should not be recovering and enjoying myself.

"If it were me," she continues, " I'd withdraw into a shell and stay in my room. I really admire you."

"Thanks, but I would rather be admired for some unusual and exciting sexual exploits and adventures rather than for being an exemplary widow. My secret wish is to get swept off my feet by some handsome Italian."

She laughs and we hang up.

I call Nancy, another friend, to see if there is any news about a memorial service. We discuss her husband's prostate cancer. She tells me I'm her role model. *I don't want to be anyone's role model. I don't want to be a widow. But there's no way to change that.* We hang up, and I take a minute to reflect on the fact that although I am a widow it no longer delineates who I am. I feel encouraged that I have moved on and not gotten stuck in the role of grieving widow.

Aboard the plane I still can't get Loren's death out of my mind. I arrive in Rome tired. I try not to let Dwayne's death interfere with my arrival, yet it is always in the back of my mind, like a lingering cough that does not go away. *Is it Dwayne's death or the reminder of Loren's death? Judy, c'mon, it's okay to have fun. After all, that was the purpose of this trip—to feel free to laugh, flirt, and join in whatever merriment comes my way.* I know that Loren would want me to play and laugh, although I certainly don't need his permission anymore . . . or do I?

Once I stop focusing on death, the trip is wonderful. The Notte Bianca—White Night—Festival, the main reason for this trip, is fabulous. There's music and entertainment all night, with the museums open for twenty-four hours. One night I have dinner at Roberto's house with his friends, after which we go first to a jazz concert, then walk through the ruins, and finally stop for drinks and coffee. Along the way I see a lot of handsome Italian men for whom I would break out a condom, but they don't see me. That's all right; just looking at men and feeling desire seems so different from two years ago. I wander into my hotel at 5 a.m., look sheepishly at the owner behind the desk, and ask, "When's breakfast?" I realize that I have not stayed up late like this since Loren died and have missed it.

For days I continue wandering through Rome. I get lost in back alleys and end up in front of a lovely shop, where I purchase a beautiful orange and yellow paisley shawl. The crowds near the Trevi Fountain jostle me as I push my way toward it. Once there, I turn my back and toss my coin into it, which, according to legend, ensures a return to this beguiling city. One day my destination is Piazza Navona, where I wander around the Bernini statues and have cappuccino. Another day I find a tiny watch shop and buy the newest Swatch watch—the band brightly colored with turquoise, orange, and black. After a visit to the Vatican, I amble through some dark lanes and purchase a lovely onyx and amber necklace. And so the days go, wandering, eating, and shopping. There are times I smile when I remember an experience Loren and I had, but at other times, as the existentialists say, I am the experience. There's something about Rome, perhaps its timelessness, which allows me to feel safe as I grapple with my difficult feelings. Rome is, after all, known as the Eternal City.

On my last night, when I'm dining by myself in a lovely little pizzeria overlooking the Coliseum, I have one of those "aha" experiences that sheds light on my thoughts and feelings about whether I will always be a widow. I realize, with a start, that in one sense I am a permanent widow and will perpetually be one. Dwayne's death and Carol's and Nancy's comments have made me comprehend that I have a responsibility to my friends still to face what I already have faced—the death of a spouse. I have knowledge they don't have, despite the fact that it was acquired unwillingly. When their spouses die, I have to share my knowledge, either by words or deeds. I realize that every time I help a friend through widowhood I will be thrown back to when Loren died and reminded of my own sadness. Perhaps the intensity will decrease, but the experience and sadness will not go away. Yet as with Dwayne's death and my conversation with Fran, I have already learned that the sadness will be fleeting and not hold me back from my new life.

A tentative smile forms on my lips. Wouldn't it be great, I think, if Loren welcomed Dwayne to wherever we go when we die, once again a mentor to him? I stroll leisurely back to the hotel, at peace, and pack for the trip home.

Back home, I put my suitcase on the bed and start unpacking. I smile as I look at the treasures I bought in Rome but also as I think about my last night there. I like the image of Loren and I continuing to be role models to our friends, in both life and death.

One year later, on the third anniversary of Loren's death, I get up early, take some ashes to the beach, throw them in the water, and watch them disappear. I take a long walk, reflect on the past three years, and realize how much I have done while still honoring Loren's memory. I have moved forward with my own life, and yet Loren remains, as he always will, a part of me.

After a noon meeting I feel the need to go home quickly and be alone. Once home, as if following some hidden script I go straight to the music cabinet and pick out five special CDs: Schubert's *Quintet in C Major*, the piece Theo played at the meeting in Germany when he was talking about Loren; Boccelli's *Sacred Arias* and the special opera collection *Songs of Love*, both of which I played at the memorial service; *The Messiah*, the music Loren played when he was sad; and Mozart's *Requiem*, which is triumphant with hope at the end. I turn the sound up very loud, sit down, and cry for hours. When the music ends, I'm surprised that I feel great—like I've been through a real cleansing process. What's more, I realize that I was sitting in the spot where Loren always sat as he blasted *The Messiah* and cried, either about work or someone's death. *These anniversaries are so powerful.*

It seems impossible that it has been already three years since Loren's death, I think, as I lie in bed exhausted but not worn out. I reflect on the progress I've made in this journey through grief with the aid of "tincture of time." In addition to the early concrete experiences of cooking for myself, traveling, and having fun, and the recent sexual stirrings, I now really care about life and, most importantly, look forward to the future, even one without Loren. Still I can't ever imagine forgetting Loren's death day. But who knows? I never thought I would forget my dad's death day, and yet the year that Loren died the date passed unnoticed until a week later.

I think about my dad and Loren, the deaths of the two most important men in my life. I remember that after a certain point the pictures of my dad seemed alien because he was so much in my heart. This is happening with Loren also. Not that I don't think of Loren a lot, but he's so much a part of me now that I don't need pictures anymore. It frightens me, but I know this process is necessary. The last time I was up in Palo Alto at Connie's house I was startled when I saw a picture of Loren on her table. Although I knew it was Loren, he somehow wasn't my Loren anymore. I still get worried that I will lose the memory of him, but after three years I'm less worried and know I have to live my life.

I stop thinking about the anniversary, put on some soft music, and drift off to sleep. I need my sleep because tomorrow I plan to take my granddaughter, Marley, now six and three-quarters years old, on an overnight trip to see dolphins in their natural habitat. Part of my new life is being an active grandmother. I realize with a start that although Loren knew Marley when she was young he never had the kind of relationship I have with her now.

During the trip, Marley and I have a grand time. We laugh, hold hands, swim in the pool, eat Chinese food then ice cream, and she says, with the enthusiasm unique to children, "Grandma Judy, this hotel (the Holiday Inn Express) is the most beautiful hotel in the whole world."

Marley has trouble falling asleep, like her mom. I remember how Loren used to tell Missy to keep picturing a beautiful place, like a field filled with flowers, until she fell asleep. I tell Marley the same thing, and it works. I think of Loren, look at Marley, and feel lucky, despite my loss. My life is full.

I think about how I used to wonder whether I would be a permanent widow and realize I don't worry about that anymore. For a while I was the spitting image of the woman in a black dress never enjoying life after the death of her husband. I have not remained that way. Still, I will always be the kind of permanent widow who helps other new widows and widowers and will always miss Loren. Besides, I've decided that being a permanent widow is a state of mind not a literal role.

I get home just in time to change and get ready to go to the racetrack with Connie. *The racetrack is a perfect metaphor for my life right now.*

While waiting for her to arrive, I continue to dream about future possibilities. I know I will never find anyone like Loren, but maybe in the future I will meet someone I can have fun with or who can replace the battery-operated penis with a live one. I realize that if I never meet another man I will still enjoy myself and have a full life. On the other hand, perhaps on my next trip I will sit next to a gorgeous hunk who will sweep me off my feet, or maybe at home I will meet someone in Starbucks, or at the Italian bar where I occasionally eat, or even in the Italian class I will start next week.

Maybe a long shot will come in some day. Who knows? As at the race-track, it depends on who is running.

# About the Author

JUDY SCHREIBER-MOSHER WAS BORN IN BROOKLYN, NEW YORK, AND GREW UP in Rockaway Beach, Long Island. A graduate of Smith College, she attended Columbia University, where she obtained her training in occupational therapy. After moving to Washington, D.C., and working for fifteen years as an occupational therapist, she enrolled at Howard University, graduated with a master's degree in social work, and began her second career, as a Licensed Clinical Social Worker and psychotherapist. Employed in this capacity for twenty-eight years by the National Institute of Mental Health, she specialized in working with people diagnosed with schizophrenia.

In 1996, Judy and her late husband, Dr. Loren Mosher, moved to San Diego, California. An adjunct faculty member at San Diego State University, she taught master's degree social work students strategies for treating the persistently mentally ill. Still residing in San Diego, she continues to practice as a psychotherapist while embarking on her third career—writing. Her work has been published in *Seasons of Life*, a national newsletter sponsored by VITAS Healthcare Corporation; *Self-Growth Newsletter*; and the *San Diego Union Tribune*.

# Order Form

**Quantity**                                                                 **Amount**

_____*Tincture of Time: Living Through Grief to Hope* ($14.00)      _____

_____*How to Cope with the Death of a Partner: Strategies for Surviving*
*the Difficult Times Ahead and Maintaining Your Emotional Health*
($7.50)                                                                         _____

_____ *Remembrance Calendar* ($9.95)                                         _____

Sales tax of 8.75% for California residents _____

Shipping and handling ($3.00 for first book; _____

$2.00 for first booklet; _____

$2.75 for first calendar; _____

$1.00 for each additional item)_____

**Total Amount Enclosed** _____

## Quantity discounts available

| |
|---|
| **Method of payment:** |
| ❏ Check or money order enclosed (made payable to **Soteria Press** in US funds only) |
| ❏ MasterCard    ❏ VISA |
| Credit Card#:_____Exp.:_____ |

**Ship to (please print):**

Name _____

Address _____

City/State/Zip _____

Phone_____

2616 ANGELL AVENUE, SAN DIEGO, CA 92122
PHONE/FAX 858-550-0312
WWW.SOTERIAPRESS.COM